Waiting for a Song in the Night:
The Trauma of Pastoral Termination

Eli Landrum

Parson's Porch Books

Waiting for a Song in the Night
ISBN: Softcover 978-1-946478-07-8
Copyright © 2017 by Eli Landrum.

All rights reserved. No part of this book may be reproduced or transmitted in any form or by any means, electronic or mechanical, including photocopying, recording, or by any information storage and retrieval system, without permission in writing from the publisher.

To order additional copies of this book, contact:

Parson's Porch Books
1-423-475-7308
www.parsonsporch.com

Parson's Porch Books is an imprint of Parson's Porch & Company (PP&C) in Cleveland, Tennessee. PP&C is an innovative company which raises money by publishing books of noted authors, representing all genres. All donations from contributors and profits from publishing are shared with the poor.

*To Barbara,
whose love and support enrich my life
beyond measure*

Contents

Introduction	7
Chapter 1: To the Brink: A Personal Odyssey	13
Chapter 2: The Dimensions of Darkness	21
Chapter 3: Help to Walk and Not Faint	39
Chapter 4: Causes of Crises	52
Chapter 5: A Defective Approach	73
Chapter 6: Elements of Hope	86
Epilogue	102

Introduction

"Men cry out under a load of oppression;
they plead for relief from the arm of the powerful.
But no one says, 'Where is God my Maker,
who gives songs in the night'" (Job 35:9-10).

"By day the Lord directs his love,
at night his song is with me—
a prayer to the God of my life" (Ps. 42:8).

"I thought about the former days,
the years of long ago;
I remembered my songs in the night.
My heart mused and my spirit inquired:
'Will the Lord reject forever?
Will he never show his favor again?'" (Ps. 77:5-7).[1]

Life has exhilarating moments when the spirit soars and the heart sings out of pure, unrestrained joy. A person experiences such elation, peace, and satisfaction that music—or at least some semblance of melody—seems to be the only appropriate response. So, in monotone, on perfect pitch, or somewhere in between, the soul sings its happy expressions of praise, gratitude, and sheer celebration of life that, for the moment, is good. Often, spontaneous songs that well up from life's depths are addressed to God in answer to His grace and goodness.

Conversely, life also has dark moments when the heart cannot sing. The spirit can produce no melody; and the words of song cannot get around, over, or under a large lump in the throat. Life inspires no rhymes. A long night of the soul settles in and presses down on life with its inky, suffocating darkness. In a blackness almost physical in denseness, no song comes to lips drawn tight by anxiety's strain and by tension's taut pull. An individual has come

---

[1] Unless otherwise indicated, Scripture quotes are from the *New International Version of the Holy Bible*, Copyright 1985 by The Zondervan Corporation.

to the point where God gives no song in the night; in fact, God seems to be absent or, at best, the great, silent Spectator.

As I write, scattered across my denomination's landscape are pastors in various stages of pilgrimages of pain. They struggle through a seemingly endless night with no song to sing. They comprise a society of sufferers, bound together in a brotherhood by the burden they bear. These pastors are facing increasing pressure to resign immediately or by a set date, regardless of whether they have a place to go. Some have been told they are being terminated. Their churches—or groups of leaders who hold the power—have decided and decreed that the pastors' tenures have come to a screeching halt. Often, the verdicts are delivered in the name of the Lord, piously phrased in self-assured religious dialect.

The pastoral victims' names are legion. Many laypeople would be shocked to know the number of pastors who face termination each week across the Southern Baptist Convention. People genuinely concerned about ministerial leaders would be dismayed at some churches' treatment of pastors. How many pastors per day fall in the religious arena? People in the pews would be surprised. According to statistics supplied by the Church Administration Department of the (then) Baptist Sunday School Board, a survey revealed that in 1984, 1,056 pastors had been terminated, a rate of 88 each month. In 1988, a similar survey showed that 1,392 pastors annually were terminated, about 116 pastors each month— almost four pastors a day and an increase of 28 per month from the 1984 survey. Again, according to compiled statistics, in 54 percent of the cases involving serious church conflicts, the pastor left or had to leave. In 1999, 72,000 pastors and clergy were fired across America for various reasons. In some cases, the pastors were partially at fault; but in others, they were not at fault. Yet they and their families were pinked-slipped and shown the door.

By 1999 terminations of pastors and full-time church staff members among Southern Baptists leveled off somewhat. Across 26 state conventions, 1077 full-time pastors, bivocational pastors and full-time staff members were terminated. In 2000, the number declined to 987, still an average of more than two per day. The 1999 survey indicated that only 55 percent of pastors who experienced forced termination returned to church-related vocations while 45 percent did not.

In 2011, Thom Rainer, president of LifeWay Christian Resources, reported that during the previous seven years, about 1.5% of senior pastors were terminated each year, a seven-year total of 10.5%. During that seven-year stretch, a senior pastor serving a church had one chance in 10 of being terminated.[2] Church-related ministries, and pastoral ministry in particular, have become increasingly dangerous and uncertain vocations.

By and large, pastors who become victims of forced termination struggle under most church members' radar. These hurting wounded answered what they felt to be God's genuine call to pastoral ministry. Many of them spent years preparing themselves to be the best possible pastors. Some paid a high price in self-sacrifice and lean times of barely getting by financially to get an education. Most, if not all, felt divinely called to their present places of service. Then, with shocking suddenness, the scattered clouds in their ministerial skies have gathered, darkened, and lowered. The threatening roll of thunder has replaced the trumpet call and organ music. What were familiar sanctuaries where they led worship experiences have become stained-glass arenas where they are engaged in a grim struggle to survive against imposing odds.

I feel for and with pastors who face the looming specter of forced termination. My ministerial near-death experience has enabled me to relate to them deeply. I know what being pushed to the brink is like. I came close enough to the cliff's edge to peer anxiously and nervously into the abyss, and the experience shook the foundations of my life. I have the deepest respect and admiration for people who continue to give their best in their pastoral ministries and who live constantly with the real possibility of sudden, shattering forced termination.

For years, I have wished for a forum in which to state with emphatic clarity: Pastors are human beings with real feelings! They are fallible and flawed, people with feet of clay on pilgrimage with others who also have feet of clay. Pastors make mistakes. They

---

[2] Statistics taken from the LifeWay Christian Resources website.

have problems, concerns, and questions. They bleed real blood when they are slashed; they bruise when blows are landed; they churn inside when people they love are hurt. Pastors have no divine protection from trouble; they receive no noticeable favoritism from God. As far as I have been able to determine, no mysterious, divine figure appears in their fiery furnaces where some perish in the flames of anger and unconcern, and no angels show up in their lions' dens to shut tight the predators' mouths.

I have known some pastors who sang or fashioned some semblance of melody as they made their ministerial rounds. For the time being, all the brush fires were out; and for the moment all the lids seemed to be staying on. I have known many, however, who waited in anguished silence for a dawn they feared might not come. Rising from deep inside was a silent scream that protested the darkness. They could not sing the Lord's song in the strange land of menacing threat and deepening gloom. They reached a trembling, searching hand for the unseen hand of One whom they trusted was in the shadows, watching over His own. They had preached sermons urging their congregations to have faith and courage in tough times, assuring believers of God's presence in crises. In their own pastoral crises, they clung doggedly to that deepest belief of their lives.

To pastoral strugglers who desperately are trying to make sense of the shattered pieces of their world, I dedicate this book with a deep sense of kinship and with a fervent prayer that one day, they will be able to sing again. I also offer this effort to church folk who can draw the best from their pastors, elevate the pastoral role, and stem the rising tide of pastoral terminations.

This book is intensely personal and confessional in nature. I understand and accept the risks involved in relating deeply personal experiences. I am willing to risk putting a great deal of myself "out there" for readers to see because of the objective: to move people to consider seriously the impact and the implications of terminating pastors without just cause. The goal is worth the price to me. I have no desire to be seen as a near martyr; and I am not looking for sympathy for a long, painful ordeal. Deepest sympathy needs to be reserved for pastors who have become severely wounded casualties struggling toward recovery. They have suffered trauma more shattering than mine. The word *trauma* is defined as "an injury or wound violently produced....an emotional experience, or shock, which has a lasting psychic effect."³ Pastoral termination—and the pressing threat of it—produce lasting, devastating effects.

I do not write to get back at or expose anyone. I would like to make some small contribution to restoring a strong sense of God's leading churches and pastors in the beginning and the ending of pastoral tenures. The sense of call, of divine guidance, needs to be recognized and respected in pastor-church, pastor-staff, and church-staff relationships. In many ways, this book is intended to be a highly personal plea that we—pastors and laypeople alike—regain a lofty view of God's presence, will, and direction in pastoral tenures.

---

³ *Webster's New World Dictionary of the American Language: College Edition,* p. 1550.

Chapter 1

To the Brink: A Personal Odyssey

In the Beginning

The night remains forever focused sharply in my memory. At will, I can recall the sights and sounds that still bring feelings of pleasure. It was the night of my first attempt to deliver a sermon. I was 19 years old, and an immature and somewhat introverted sophomore-to-be in college. I had made a tentative, hesitant step toward committing my life to the pastoral ministry in answer to what I deemed to be God's call. My pastor—a rotund, kindly man who had helped me along my difficult way toward a decision about my life's work—had asked me to "preach" during the Wednesday evening prayer service. I worked had on that first message. I used almost everything I had heard or read about the Isaiah passage I had chosen. I searched for and included every illustration that remotely applied. Painstakingly, I wrote the sermon in longhand and put it in a loose-leaf binder so I could take it with me to the pulpit. If stage-fright should seize me, I could resort to reading to avoid total embarrassment.

The big night came all too quickly. My moment of truth arrived. The pastor introduced me to people who had known me practically all my life. I stepped to the pulpit with my manuscript clutched tightly in my hand. A torrent of adrenaline pumped furiously through my body, which felt like all nerves that were tightly drawn. Amazingly, with trembling legs and dry mouth, I readily recalled what I wanted to say and said it without a major disaster. I was as surprised as anyone. When I finished saying everything I knew in 15 minutes or less, the pastor said something to the effect that he wished he had done as well in his first sermon. Then, the people in the small group came by to shake my hand, hug me, and compliment me in warm, glowing terms. I felt exhilarated! I did not have enough sense to realize the pastor was being kind and that had I fallen on my face that night, those people would have picked me up gently, brushed me off, and said that no one ever had done it better or more gracefully. I was one of them; in a real sense, I was theirs. They were with me, and they were for me.

Later, I could not stay at home. I could not be still. I felt I had won a major victory, with divine help; and such a triumph demanded celebration. Parenthetically, you need to know that my celebrations never have come within hailing distance of being wild and colorful. On the night of my high school graduation, I opted not to join a number of my fellow graduates in going to a nearby larger city to celebrate. I walked from the high school auditorium toward home. On the way, I stopped a local drive-in where I once had worked. I savored a soft drink and a pack of crackers—alone. Then I walked home at an outrageously decent hour and went to bed.

On the night of my successful start toward renown in the religious realm, I went for a walk. I strolled down by the grammar school, along the short gravel road that led by the football field, toward the high-school gym. On that special night I sang—loudly and off-key, but joyously. I remember singing all the words I knew of the song "My God and I," and I sang them over and over. We would walk through all my fields together, hand in hand as good friends do. As I mentally looked down the long road ahead, I was confident the journey would be good. With God taking care of me while I worked for Him, the future held no threats or fears.

In my moments of happy, naive euphoria, I never dreamed that one day the music would die—or refuse to be born. I could not have imagined that for an agonizingly long stretch in my life, I would have no song to sing in the longest, darkest night I would endure. In that period, how often I longed to recapture the feeling of that long-ago night when God was at my side—so much mine, so reassuring, so real and supportive. In the beginning, the thought never occurred to me that someday, I would not be able to bring myself to join my congregation in singing the hymn "God Will Take Care of You." I choked on the words, for I had no real sense of God's care.

The journey from the night of happy song to the night of anguished silence was long and demanding. It had its hills and valleys, twists and turns, rough stretches and smooth going. I often have reflected on the long, winding path from song to silence. Measured in miles, the trip would take less than a day over good roads. Measured in time and effort, it involved years and immeasurable energy. All along the way, I met nothing I could not handle with God's help and the assistance of supportive people.

On the Way

The story of my journey from night of glad song to extended night of perplexed, painful, tuneless silence is not especially colorful or exciting. Its uniqueness lies in its being mine and its being different from anyone else's pilgrimage. I made my public commitment to the pastoral ministry on a bright Sunday morning immediately before my junior year in college. In front of people who had known me, taught me, cared for me, nurtured me to my earlier profession of faith Christ, and supported me in my somewhat halting route to the point of life-altering choice, I shared my decision. God was calling me to church-related vocation, and I was answering.

I remained in college where I had been pursuing a pre-engineering course of study. I changed my major to the area the school recommended: religion and philosophy. I made the switch with some reservations, but it turned out to be one of the most rewarding experiences of my academic journey. My major professor was a brilliant, conservative Lutheran pastor-scholar who saw no paradox in a religious person who could think logically and clearly. He prepared me superbly for what would be a lengthy, challenging stint in seminary. He made me think and demanded that I put my thoughts into writing that was understandable and to the point. I still remember one of his favorite sayings as he prepared us for one of his thorough exams: "The test will be made up of discussion questions. Shoot with a rifle, not a shotgun!" He taught me to organize my thoughts and to put them on paper. He helped remove the fear of discussion questions. Little did I know at the time what a great contribution he was making to my life and ministry.

I increased my course load, continued to work during the summers, and finished college early. I worked at the jobs available in my small hometown and looked forward to the time when I would go to New Orleans, Louisiana, to enter seminary. Finally, the day arrived; and I made another of the multiple beginnings that would occur in my life.

As the car in which my mother and cousin had brought me to New Orleans Baptist Theological Seminary pulled away, I had the feeling of being on my own for the first time—and of being terribly alone and unsure. I was in the largest city I ever had seen, much less lived in; I was at a new school where I knew few people; and I faced my biggest academic challenge. Mercifully, I was unaware I was entering the most difficult year of my life to that point. Had I known, I likely would have caught the retreating car and gone back home.

To my dismay, I discovered I was housed in what once had been the garden district of New Orleans in a dormitory that was a relic of another era. The seminary had moved across the city into sparkling new quarters but had retained the one facility in the old location to house men who could not be placed in dorms on campus. Without a car, I was faced with finding daily transportation across town to the seminary. I literally would have to commute to class! To compound my situation, almost immediately I got a job pumping gas at a large department store's service station near the seminary campus. This meant a nightly city-bus trip back across town to my dorm room. I went to class and worked in one location, and I slept—literally about all I did—in a distant location. My seminary career was not exactly off to a promising start.

The first four months of my first year in seminary were the most difficult months of my life to that point. I had almost no time to relax. I started out taking a full course load, working 30-plus hours at the service station, and taking part in an all-day mission trip on Sundays to the jumping-off place in extreme southern Louisiana, the only way I could meet the seminary's missions requirement. I had little time for study or for rest. I felt I had no room to breathe.

In the stifling atmosphere in which I found myself, I became discouraged. At an extremely low point in the early months of seminary life, I wrote to my mother and poured out my semi-despair. Her answering letter gave me hope and impetus to push on toward my goal. She expressed a confidence in me I did not have in myself and badly needed; she stated clearly and lovingly that she felt I would do something good and fine with my life. She was sure I would accomplish something worthwhile. I kept her words handy for quick recall when the going became rough and the way unclear—and uncertain.

At mid-year, the long-awaited and desperately hoped-for news came: a room was available for me on campus. I would be near my classes and my work. I also decided to lighten my class load and make up the slack during summer school. To do so meant I would graduate in the summer after my entering class graduated in the spring. That decision turned out to be one of the best I could have made. I felt that a great weight had been lifted from my shoulders. I emerged from the deep gloom of my temporary dark age and basked in new-found light and warmth. I felt a freedom I had not known for a long and tiring length of time.

I have chronicled in summary form the dark period of my early seminary experience to stress several points I need to make clear. First, I have not described hardship to generate sympathy or to pat myself on the back. Many fellow students had a far rougher time than I and are to be commended for their sacrifices to obtain the training they wanted and needed to be better-equipped ministers. My hat is off to many men who worked 40 hours a week at nighttime jobs to support their families and to wives who worked full-time to help their student husbands. Most of us acquired first-hand knowledge of hard times and bone weariness. My almost joyless stretch of life, however, was nothing in comparison with what I would face in a few short years. Nothing in my experience prepared me for the prolonged night without song I would be forced to endure.

A second point I need to make is that during college summers and seminary days I was introduced to hard work on a consistent basis. I looked forward to working in a church-related vocation, and I expected to work. I do not recall ever expecting a church to make possible an easy ride for me—to provide a more-than-adequate salary for minimal work. In fact, I intended to earn respect by the manner in which I went about my job. Had I harbored any tendency in the direction of thinking I could glide along as a privileged minister, it would have vaporized at the beginning of my first day on the first job I had in a church.

Finally, I never expected a church to restore the years the locusts had eaten. I did not feel churches I would serve needed to make up for the lean years I had known while I was preparing myself for ministry. I do recall looking forward to the day when I would not have to count my pennies and allot myself a daily food allowance. I promised myself that someday, I would eat a really good meal now and then. I would allow myself to splurge occasionally. During ensuing and better years, my early habit of ordering the lowest-priced meals on restaurants' menus was hard to break. In seminary, I looked forward to better times financially, but I did not feel anybody owed me anything. I wanted a chance to work at what I felt God had called me to do. I suppose I felt the only thing my denomination owed me was a chance to implement God's calling.

My hunch is that the vast majority of pastoral ministers share much of my experience and my feelings. Many of them forged ahead through rough stretches and worked hard; they did so gladly for the opportunity to fulfill their calling. Some may have had money, or well-off families, or generous benefactors. Most of the men I knew, however, were doing what I was doing—scratching and clawing toward a goal we felt was worthwhile. I found that sometimes such desert stretches are merely preludes to wider wildernesses.

Descent of Darkness

Looking back, I always am amazed at how quickly the music ended and the light went out in my ministerial world—and nearly in the entirety of my world. The sudden eclipse of my sun was stunning. I had encountered difficulties in the pastoral ministry on which I had embarked; I had dealt with problem people, individuals who had disliked and opposed me, and delicate situations in churches. Yet with the unexpected swiftness of a blown light bulb, I was reduced to making my way tenuously in a darkness where danger lurked and where I could be hurt badly.

I was not derelict in my duties as a pastor. I was not inaccessible; I did not golf, hunt, fish, or leave town frequently. I did not take or waste the church's money. I was not immoral and did not conduct a questionable lifestyle. I did not mismanage my salary or fail to pay my bills. Instead, during my fourth year as pastor I was blindsided during an attempt to resolve conflict that threatened the church's fellowship and ministry.

A church staff member and a lay leader were having relationship issues. I asked the individuals involved to meet with me and agreed with the lay leader's stipulation that the chairman of deacons be present. During the discussion, the staff member expressed a willingness to do whatever would satisfy the lay leader's expectations. The lay leader responded rather sternly, was not open to negotiation, and finally stormed out of the meeting. Instead of resolving the conflict, I became the focal point of the lay leader's anger and hostility. I had not taken the right side in the dispute. A later meeting in my office with the lay leader produced nothing positive. I subsequently learned that the magic words would have been an apology to the lay leader for perceived grave offenses.

I had intended to end conflict; instead, I became entangled in conflict. I had meant to help ease tension and prevent disharmony so the church's work could proceed smoothly. The result was my beginning to experience a degree of tension I had never known. I became the object of unrelenting, growing pressure that at any moment might force me out of my pastorate with no place to go. For the first time, I stared into the cold, cruel eyes of raw, real threat to myself and to the three people for whom I felt deep and total responsibility. My wife and two small children had become potential victims along with me.

Chapter 2

The Dimensions of Darkness

I suppose that to some extent I am a wordsmith. I have preached, taught, and written a great deal. I spent years as an editor of manuscripts. Yet I confess I have difficulty finding the right words to express what I experienced when night fell and the music died with alarming suddenness in my relatively peaceful world. I feel some sense of frustration at trying to convey the agony of my long night of waiting for some pale shaft of light and some dim note of melody to signal the dawn of hope and joy. The psalmist wrote that "weeping may remain for a night, but rejoicing comes in the morning" (Ps. 30:5). He neglected to mention, however, how long the night might be or how deep the darkness one might have to endure. To me, eternity can be defined as anxious, endless straining to see the first soft rays of morning to signal the new beginning one fears may not come.

I do not recall that I ever cried. At least, I do not remember weeping. My eyes may have misted briefly in anger or in momentary relief, but I never broke down and wept as I had done at times over the years. The emotion behind crying was there, deep down in my gut, many times. I certainly felt the stirrings, the empty feeling in the pit of my stomach, the lost feeling of facing elements over which I had no control. I joined a numberless band of people who know what living with emotional pain over an extended period of time means. That kind of pain is every bit as real as physical pain; it is sharp and searing; and it dulls and lessens life. Emotional pain drains life's energies because it is all-consuming; it is always there. A medically-trained friend has said that emotional pain affects every organ and system in the body.

I have not had to endure a great amount of physical pain. Years ago, I developed kidney stones, at least two of them. I had ministered to people who had them, and I had tried to sympathize with them. Yet I had no remote clue concerning the degree of pain a tiny, internal sand spur could inflict until one played side-and-seek in one of my kidneys. When it decided to move, I had to move. The pain began as a dull ache in my side and grew more intense until all I could do was pace the floor. The hurting became all-consuming; my only thought was to get to my doctor, to receive medication to relieve the pain, to have the stone found and removed. My body and brain screamed for relief. That pain has been the most severe I have endured. I cannot conceive of any greater pain. I never want to hurt like that again. If that pain can be compared with the pain of childbirth, as I have been told, my respect for mothers is astronomical.

I have come to view the worst physical pain I have experienced as an appropriate parallel to or analogy of the emotional pain I felt during the extended threat of forced termination. I knew—and my wife and I faced the fact squarely—that only a thin, tenuous thread held back the people who wanted us gone. The real possibility was that at any moment, we literally could be out on the street. We lived with that harsh reality—a fiendish, unwelcome, tenacious intruder—for more than two years.

Even now, as I write these words in a comfortable study, far removed by time and distance from my harrowing experience, the memories still are painful and stir deep emotions. The pain has lessened greatly with the passing of years, but the memories will stay with me for life. I remember long walks alone, moments staring into starlit heavens trying to reach a distant God, anguished prayers, sleepless hours, and anxious pursuit of available alternatives that offered flickering candlelight flames of hope. I did not want, expect, or ask for a larger church, a step up; I wanted out. Repeatedly, I said to a God I desperately hoped was listening that all I wanted was relief for me and my family. The deep appreciation I had developed for Job across the years was taking on new elements of intimate identification.

During my long night without song, the Psalms and I became good friends. I began to identify more closely with and understand more clearly the transparently human hymnists who were bluntly honest in their struggles. I asked their questions with them: "Why, O Lord, do you stand far off? Why do you hide yourself in times of trouble" (Ps. 10:1)? "How long, O Lord? Will you forget me forever? How long will you hide your face from me?" (Ps. 13:1). "My God, my God, why have you forsaken me? Why are you so far from saving me, so far from the words of my groaning?" (Ps. 22:1). With the psalmist, I knew what being "a wineskin in the smoke" (Ps. 119:83) felt like. I also experienced the poet's feeling that people were plowing his back, making their furrows long (Ps. 129:3).

I never quite reached the depths to which the writer of Psalm 109 plummeted. He prayed that his opponent's days would be few, that his enemy's children would be fatherless and his wife a widow, and that no one would extend kindness to his enemy or have pity on his children. He asked that his opponent's children would be vagabonds and beggars and that the enemy's posterity and memory would be blotted out. I never prayed that the people besieging me have their teeth broken in their mouths, as the psalmist did in Psalm 58:6. To be honest, I came close a few times, but I managed to avoid a desire for vengeance. I did want to be vindicated of false charges against me. I wanted the truth to be known about accusations circulating concerning my conduct in the conflict meeting. Yet more than that, I wanted to be freed from unrelenting pressure that was squeezing dry my life and the lives of the people dearest to me.

The range of emotions I experienced were incredibly broad and came in continuous waves. The emotions were repeated much as scales a voice or a piano student rehearses over and over. As I look back, some of what I experienced must have been extreme fatigue from dealing constantly with all the feelings that raw, relentless threat triggered. Some days, I dreaded getting up and facing a new day through which I would struggle to survive. I prayed for another time, another place. I wanted a few—actually, a lot—less of the emotions with which I wrestled.

Fear

One primary emotion I had to name, acknowledge, and face squarely was *fear* that sometimes verged on terror—stark, surging fear that I would be fired. My wife and I agreed that if only the two of us had been involved, we could have walked away and never have looked back. She was qualified to teach or to work in the business arena, and she had experience in the job market. I had equipped myself to be a pastor or teacher, but I had a few other marginal "marketable skills." We could make it. Yet with two small children who were dependent on us, the risk factor in resigning with no place to go would be great.

Of course, I was dealing with the fear of failure. Forced termination would mean to me, and probably to many other people, that I had failed. The strong signal might be sent that I could not "hack it"; that I could not stick it out; that I could not manage, cope, and relate. Furthermore, if I were fired, how many other churches would be interested in calling me as pastor—or even as a staff member? Would termination mean the end of my pastoral ministry, to which I felt called and to which I was willing to invest my life under God's leading? I feared for the future, for my family, for my "professional career." Could I make a successful transition to another vocation, if I was forced to do so as many other pastors have been forced to do? Or, would I fail at that, too?

I was (and am) all too aware that our society is obsessed with winners, with success. We have increasingly less place for losers, for people who have failed in some area. We cannot afford to fail. Yet I was staring failure full in the face, and I was deeply afraid.

Anger

In retrospect, probably the dominant emotion with which I wrestled was *anger*. Of course, I was angry with the people who were applying the constant, growing pressure. What gave them the right to subject me and my family to such unfair treatment? The sad realization came that I had worked for construction companies, a large department store chain, a small furniture factory, and a utility company; and I never had been treated with anything approaching the calculated cruelty to which I was being subjected in a church. At most, I felt I deserved a reprimand for not handling a conflict situation smoothly and well. Yet I had done nothing for which I deserved to be destroyed. I said as much, as clearly as I knew how, to people who would listen. I felt, and acknowledged, deep anger toward those who planned and orchestrated my dismissal/demise after a prolonged period of proper punishment. Did not any of them care remotely that a career, a future, a family's welfare were at stake? Did not any of them stop to think of the possible results of this deliberate overkill on four lives, not to mention the permanent damage to a church's reputation and image? And on what basis or for what cause? At most, a personality clash.

I was angry at people who could speak out, exert influence, and cause people who were applying the pressure to stop, but who did not do so. Surely, anyone who knew anything about the situation was aware that as soon as possible, I would leave. I could not remain under any circumstances, and I did not want to do so. As certainly, somebody could bring reason and caution to bear. As far as I was able to determine, little was done to ease the pressure or to determine fact from fiction. I knew the reasons then, and I am more convinced of the reasons now. Nobody would risk incurring the hostility being leveled at me; it was my problem, none of theirs. Also, the church members would be there long after I was gone; and they wanted no lingering feuds. I was temporary; they were permanent residents. In addition, I believe some people who remained outside the storm wanted to see me go and were hoping the campaign succeeded. Some literally could not afford to get involved openly on either side; they had clients and customers in the church. Others did not know what to do, did not care, or were unaware of the struggle. For a long time, I have been convinced that a large part of the church membership had no idea that sharp conflict continued. At best, they had some vague perception that something was wrong and that people were upset about something. Yet part of the rage I felt was directed at people who refused to help, who watched as I twisted in the wind.

I was angry with myself. Why had I walked into a fight that was not mine without weighing more carefully the situation and the people involved? Why had I not seen—or admitted—the capacity of some people drawn into the conflict to react quickly and strongly to my futile attempt at resolution? Why could I not escape the vise that steadily closed on me and my family?

I also was angry at God. I told Him as much. In prayer, and in some expressions that echoed the psalmists' words, I let God know (as though He did not know already) that I did not understand His absence, His silence, His lack of care. Why did He not do something, and do it quickly? Did He not know the pain my wife and I were enduring? Could He not see what continuing stress was doing to us? How could He allow those who claimed to be His people to treat others of His children as enemies to be defeated or as people who deserved punishment. Yet I continued to address God as One who heard and was able to help. As many of the psalmists had done, I repeatedly prayed that He swiftly come to our rescue.

Anxiety

Anxiety was a constant companion that made every step I took through every day. My anxiety level stayed high; it merely moved from high to higher, depending on what church members said (or were reported to have said) and the facial and body language I happened to glimpse. Deacons' meetings became mine fields I approached with great apprehension and extreme caution. After each one I weathered successfully, I felt momentary relief that for the time being, I had averted disaster.

Saturday nights became long, lonely stretches for me. Many of those nights, I tossed and turned until early morning. I began to make my bed in the den in order not to disturb my wife's sleep. I struggled with the strong feeling that tomorrow, I would be on trial again. As I stood to preach, behind me in the choir and in front of me in the congregation would be faces that made no attempt to disguise their owners' dislike and open hostility. No one but my wife and me knew that on many Sunday mornings, I walked to the pulpit with only a few hours sleep behind me, bone weary from a struggle I felt I was losing, wondering how much longer I could endure.

When I was aware a pastor search committee was present in a worship service, my anxiety went through the roof. Early in my ministry, I had adopted the practice of not pulling out of my files what I considered to be one of my best sermons when I knew a search committee would be present. In my anxiety and fear for my ministerial life, I jettisoned that resolve. I began to play to the smaller audience sitting in the congregation. Would the committee members be impressed enough to talk with me? to invite me to preach in their church in view of a call? to recommend to their church that I be invited to be their pastor? Looking back, I am reasonably certain that search committee members picked up on our anxiety as they talked with my wife and me, no matter how positive and relaxed we consciously tried to be. Whether or not they had been told of our troubles, I think they sensed the tension we felt. Anxiety turned out to be a formidable foe that laughed at our attempts to be free.

Doubt

Darting in and out of consciousness but always immediately beneath the surface was *doubt*. I began to doubt myself. Did I have the necessary skills to be an effective pastor? As pastor search committees came and went, some not lingering long and not bothering to talk, I began to question my preaching style. Did I need to shout to make emphatic points, become more animated, tell more jokes, use more and better illustrations? Maybe, just maybe, I really could not preach effectively or impressively enough. Some supportive church members offered affirmation following sermons, but their encouragement could not stem the tide of nagging doubt.

Perhaps my personality was not appealing and turned people off. What could I do to attract and please people who could have a major say in determining my future? I tried desperately to think of ways to impress people who might hold the key that would unlock the prison in which I languished as surely as if I wore shackles. I could not do much about my physical features, but I tried to be clean, neat, and well-dressed. Did something about me that I did not recognize cause search committees to pass on me?

I reexamined my call to the pastoral ministry. Had God really called me, or had I misread His direction for my life? Maybe I had chosen the route on my own or had been influenced by other people. Perhaps I had seen the pastoral ministry as a safe, insulated vocation that brought automatic acceptance, recognition, authority, and respect. If so, with a grim, forced smile I admitted the laugh was on me. If God had not called me, I was the victim of a grossly bad joke, self-inflicted or played by others. I concluded that whatever happened, God had called me; and I had answered to the best of my ability. Out of the struggle with doubt came a curious feeling that because God had called me, He surely would assume some responsibility for my circumstances and for the future. At least, I hoped that was the case. Even here, I was not sure.

My doubt extended to God. For what reason did He allow my immensely stressful situation to continue for so long? Granted, I had made mistakes and unwise decisions. I had not handled a difficulty with the insight and the maturity it demanded. Yet I never felt I had done anything to merit the severity of what was happening to me and my family. I stubbornly refused to say anything that would give credence to charges against me. I worked hard to hold on to my name, my integrity. My wife particularly had a great deal of difficulty struggling with her question concerning the reason God permitted such unfairness in His church. I wondered how God worked in such circumstances; then, I wondered whether He did anything at all. At times, I came extremely close to doubting whether He cared. *If He does*, I remember thinking, *He certainly goes to great lengths not to demonstrate it.*

Helplessness

My fear, anxiety, and doubt constantly fed a deepening sense of *helplessness*. Always before, I could figure my way out of a jam, or my parents were present to help, or friends were willing and able to assist. Yet in my continuing pastoral crisis, I literally was doing all I knew to do. I had contacted every person I knew who might be able to help me. My growing alarm had given me an aggressiveness in asking that I had not had to that point. A chaplain friend had pointed out that sometimes we as pastors did not get opportunities because we did not ask, so I was asking. I was not getting the right answers, however.

Sometimes, I felt like the caged animals I had seen at zoos, endlessly pacing the cramped dimensions of their barred prisons. The feeling was akin to dangling by a thread. I should be able to take care of myself, my wife, and our children. Somewhere, somehow, a solution had to be available that did not mean the surrender of integrity. Surely, nobody—not even a pastor—should be forced to grovel in order to survive. What more could I do? Where was the elusive answer? For the first time in my life, I had run into a blank wall, a dead end. Factors were at work over which I had no control, with no prospects of gaining control. My sense of helplessness intensified as each day brought no end in sight.

As my two-plus years' darkness lingered, my feeling of nowhere to turn and no way out grew. How had I felt when I had only the usual stresses with which to contend, when I had to deal with what I now knew to be minor inconveniences? For the life of me, I could not remember.

Loneliness

The feeling of *loneliness* intensified with the slowly passing days. My family and I had friends and family members who gave support and encouragement. Yet they could not offer a solution to our problem. Some church members expressed their friendship and support, but they could not implement a solution to my crisis. A support group helped me work through the maze of emotions. More and more, however, I saw my family members and me as cut off and surrounded, with a ring of opponents steadily closing in, tightening the noose. At any moment the oppressors thought they could terminate me, they would do so. Who would speak for the condemned? Who would put himself/herself at risk to allow us the time to find a place to go?

To me, abject loneliness was looking around a circle of deacons in my office during a meeting and trying to calculate the "fors," the "maybes," and the "dead-set againsts." One definite "for" generates gratitude for a vast minority but also a sick feeling in the pit of the pastoral stomach. Loneliness is attending a deacons' and wives' banquet and sitting alone, as my wife did in my absence toward the end. Loneliness is walking out to the pulpit on a Sunday morning, wondering how much more you can take—and how much longer you have. Loneliness is doubting that when the showdown comes, more than a small handful of people will stand beside you. My family and I lived under a lengthening and deepening shadow of isolation.

A Shrinking Sense of Self-Worth

One of the fiercest feelings with which I had to contend was *a progressive loss of a sense of self-worth*. Often I thought, *Competent people would not find themselves in such a quagmire; or if they did, they would solve the problem quickly and smoothly*. Perhaps I lacked the relationship skills that would have gathered more support through the years. Maybe the style and quality of my ministry had failed to accumulate a reserve of respect and loyalty from which I could draw. Could the truth be that I lacked the spiritual depth I should have? What did my wife and our parents really think of someone who would open the door for such a crisis? At times I did not think much of me, and I did not see how anyone else could.

Frustration

Frustration was a daily companion. Nothing seemed to work. Every direction I took turned out to be a dead-end street, a false trail. Hope would rise on tentative wings, only to be dashed to the ground in a resounding crash. No place of service became available.

On one occasion, I sat in the office of my state's director of pastor-church relations and said that I only wanted a place where my family and I could have some breathing room, not a step up to a larger church. I meant every word. No doubt, smaller churches saw me as over-qualified, while equal-sized or larger churches viewed me as incapable of producing. So, I grappled with rising frustration.

Pastor search committees came, listened, and went. Some talked, went home to compare notes and pray, and never communicated again. With each committee's passing through, my frustration grew.

Despair

As the months dragged on, I became at least casually acquainted with *despair*. I am well aware that even as "grown men don't cry," Christians never are supposed to despair. Supposedly, if you have enough faith, you can go through any crisis with a song in your heart and a smile on your face. I did not qualify as a poster-boy for that mantra.

At a particularly low point in my valley of deep shadow, and out of a support-group session, I wrote a pastor's column in the church's weekly mail-out that laid bare my feelings for anyone who cared to see and feel. In the column, I wrote:

It came as a new experience for me. It caught me off-guard, ill-prepared. I had known—and had preached—that life includes its valleys of deep shadow. I had experienced threat, stark and ugly; grief, piercing and lingering; disappointment, crushing and shattering; failure, shaming and demeaning. Yet in all these experiences, I could see shafts of light up ahead, where I could eventually emerge from gloom into sunlight and open terrain, and where I could get my bearings as I continued my pilgrimage. Then I reached the valley of despair, and I found it to be long and deep and lonely. Others were there, in the shadows, but each struggled on his own.

The valley of the shadow of despair, I found, is more like a deep ravine whose sides are towering and sheer. I tried running, only to drop in exhaustion. I tried sitting and waiting to be found, but those who passed by could not help.

What do you do when your prayers meet with silence? When no light breaks through the gloom? When hope fades and joy becomes a bad joke? One can indulge in self-pity, express anger at God, get down on himself, blame other people—all of which I did. Or, one can get up and walk on in the shadows, holding on to the trust that the One who stands at the heart of the universe is loving, confessing "Lord, I believe," asking, "Help my unbelief." It has been the most difficult thing I have done, walking in darkness, where no light broke through and the place of emerging could not be seen. I learned that one quite literally concentrates on the next step; one takes responsibility for his own life; one goes on doing the best he knows to do. I began to emerge when I decided to stay on my feet. I don't know what lies ahead. Perhaps more treks through despair. Yet I am determined to remain upright and moving, for I have discovered that on the far side of despair can lie inner strength, a new degree of maturity, and a needed sensitivity to despairing people.

Desperation

After the fact, I recognized that as months turned into years, I began struggling with a growing *desperation* that was more intense than I would admit at the time. I prayed that God would open a door—any door. I asked Him to provide a place, any place where I could make a living and provide for my family. Freedom for me had become a fading memory. Similar to a person trying to reconstruct the face of a loved one who has been gone for a lengthy period, I could not fashion the contours of freedom from debilitating stress. I did not know what not being afraid and threatened meant. I know now that, left to my own wisdom, in my desperation I could have made choices that were not good for me or for the places to which I might have gone. Today, when I read or hear of people who describe their desperation, I identify to a high degree. I have been at least to the outer edge of desperation, and I pitched my tent there for a while.

Grief

People experience *grief* when they lose someone or something they valued deeply: a parent, a spouse, a child, a marriage, a job, an opportunity, a dream, health. I grieved because I had lost friendships. I lost respect for people to whom I had been reasonably close. I found that some were not what I had thought they were. I lost self-confidence, and I lost illusions about churches and people and myself. I grieved for what once was and what might have been. I grieved because I no longer could sing "My God and I."

The lowest point for me came at a high school football game. As I have turned the experience over and over in my mind, I realize I hit bottom. As was my practice, I went to a nearby town to watch a number of my church's young people as the team played their heated rivals. Symbolic of my feeling of isolation, I sat among strangers and waited for the game to begin, but my thoughts were focused on my dilemma, as they usually were. With many of the churning emotions I have tried to describe, I agonized over finding an avenue of release, a way to free myself and my family from the suffocating weight that pressed us to the wall. Suddenly, the thought came, sharp and clear. I had a father in an adjoining state who would do anything in his power to help me, but he could do nothing to relieve or to change my situation. I had a Heavenly Father who has all power; I was His child, and I had asked Him repeatedly for a chance to live free again. I had met only silence. Why did He not care as much for me as the concerned man in my little hometown who always had stood by me? I had hit rock bottom, as down as I ever had been in my life.

The high intensity of my feelings and the constant struggle with the broad range of emotions had a ripple effect on my family. My wife and I often found ourselves playing the game of "Ain't It Awful," lamenting our situation but so emotionally interdependent we were unable to help each other to any appreciable degree. Any affront or threat to one of us caught us both up in the strong tendency to identify, protect, and defend. Together, we tried to make sense of what was happening—to understand the causes, the hostility I had triggered, and the push to drive us away.

Our son was a baby; thus, he was spared much of the tension in which we lived. Our daughter was preschool age, and she picked up our anxiety. On the night of what we continue to call "The Great Deacons' Meeting," a meeting I am convinced was called to show me the shortest route out of town, I was getting ready to enter the arena. Paul's words about fighting beasts at Ephesus (1 Cor. 15:32) aptly described the situation as I saw it. I was trying to reassure my wife (and me) as much as possible, and she was trying to encourage me. She felt helpless; all she could do was to wait. After I left, she was in the kitchen, crying. Our little daughter came in and asked what was the matter. My wife tried to pass the situation off as lightly as she could. Our daughter, in the instinctive insight God gives little children, said in essence: "Some bad people are being mean to my daddy, aren't they?" She knew, because she understood part of what she had overheard, and she felt the tension. Added to the burden of dealing with our deep feelings was our attempt to shield our children, to protect them from wounds that would leave scars, to provide a pleasant atmosphere where laughter and joy were dominant elements. Yet to fake the music was hard, and to arrange discord into believable melody was impossible. I survived the dreaded meeting and plodded on.

I remain convinced that two trump cards I held forestalled the determination of a majority of deacons to show me the church door in the called meeting. One I had not recognized and pleasantly surprised me. Over the space of about four-years' ministry, I had forged and strengthened strong bonds with older adults in the church. I consistently visited homebound members. In one case, the elderly husband was able to attend church services, but his wife could not do so. I visited them regularly. They were long-time and highly respected members of the church. He had been a leading "pillar" and was revered. When he learned I was being pressured to leave and in danger of being terminated, he called a younger deacon and expressed his strong objection to what was happening. In essence, he stated that he was shocked deacons would treat their pastor in that manner. I believe his and other senior adults' support of me made some deacons back off a little.

The second trump card was one I held close to the vest until I discovered the deacons' intention to fire me. One night before the meeting, I called a deacon I felt (wrongly, as it turned out) I could trust and asked him to meet me and to discuss the conflict in which I was embroiled. As we drank coffee and talked, he revealed that the meeting's purpose was to terminate me. Earlier, as the conflict intensified, I had determined that if the deacons tried to force me to resign, I would take the decision to the church as a whole. At a crucial point in my conversation with the deacon, I told him as much. Either as a stroke of luck or as divine guidance, the timing was perfect. In shocked surprise, he responded that the deacons had the authority to fire me if they chose. I countered that the deacon body had not called me as pastor; the church as a whole had done so. Therefore, members of the congregation would determine my fate. Doubtless, he spread the word, and the deacons' reluctance to publicize the conflict and their intention held them at bay long enough for me to explore options to relocate.

Two lessons emerged from my survival. First, a pastor's careful attention to and discharge of his/her pastoral duties will build good will and credibility with at least a segment of a congregation. The pastor does not minister to people to stockpile I.O.U.'s to call in if and when trouble arises, but faithful ministry will build solid relationships and loyal support. Second, and sadly, a pastor must find protective leverage to call into play when he/she is threatened without just cause. These two elements played vital roles in my survival.

Not long after I wrote the pastor's column on despair, I received an opportunity to move to an incredible area of ministry. It was not merely a way out of difficulty but an opportunity beyond my wildest hope. After I moved, two letters were forwarded to me from my former church. My column on despair had appeared in the state Baptist newspaper, and two readers responded. One letter was an attempt to straighten me out theologically. The writer's thesis was that Christians do not experience despair; mine was evidence that I did not know the Bible and had not tapped available spiritual resources. Evidently I had frightened her. To this day, my strong hunch is that she was a direct descendant of one of Job's friends. The second letter was from a hospital chaplain who understood me and stated he could wish for and relate to a pastor who shared his feelings so openly and honestly. His response meant a great deal to me; it helped me continue to cope with a still-fresh brush with disaster.

My opportunity for a new beginning came, and it was a better chance than I could have drawn up. I still have the sheets from a calendar pad on which I recorded sermon topics, appointments, weddings, funerals, and so on. In the space for the day on which I received the job offer and my new beginning, above some regularly scheduled activities are words in bold, black ink: **Free at last!** On that day, I received word that the employment opportunity I had wanted so desperately and thought I had lost was mine. In the calendar space for the day before I drove out of town to a future, I wrote in the same stark black ink: **Exodus!** My leaving was precisely that: release, rescue, deliverance to a better place. The Old Testament exodus took on a whole new dimension of meaning for me. The Hebrew concept of salvation as spaciousness, wideness, roominess to live free became clearer than ever before in my experience. I left threat and pressure to begin a new life, quite literally. The words I wrote on my calendar pad expressed my feelings exactly when I wrote them, and they still do. I had then, and I have now, no better words to convey my feelings. Through the ensuing years, I periodically have taken the calendar sheet out of my file, and each time I do the bold, black words stir feelings of appreciation that are beyond my ability to express. Stronger than all the emotions with which I struggled for so long is the feeling of gratitude I have expressed to God repeatedly.

The bright rays of dawn finally penetrated the darkness of my night without song. The dictionary definition of an odyssey is "any extended wandering or journey."[4] In terms of time and miles traveled, my moving from a happy celebration on a clear night to a

---

[4] *Webster's New World Dictionary of the English Language: College Edition*, p. 1018.

darkness so deep and oppressive that grief and anger were dominant emotions was an extended journey. At times it was more wandering in the dark than it was purposeful movement toward a clearly defined goal. I learned a great deal, much of it the hard way. Yet now, with Joseph of old I can say: "You intended to harm me, but God intended it for good" (Gen. 50:20).

I received an opportunity to go to something that offered wider challenge and greater use of whatever gifts I have. I would enter a scope of ministry I never dreamed would be available. The Sunday I resigned my church, my one deacon friend, whom I love and respect highly, recommended that the church accept my resignation. He had told me in advance that he wanted the motion to come from a friend in love rather than from an enemy in hate and relief. Some who shook my hand after the service ended were not as much glad for me as they were relieved that the war was over and that they could go on their way in peace. The church gave me and my family no reception. At least the people running the show were honest in opting not to do so: they wanted nothing to do with a show of appreciation they did not feel. The church's gift for six-and-one-half years' service was one week's salary. Yet the people who had pushed us to the brink and had been poised to push us over were not to enjoy the last laugh.

Some friends in the church had become fully aware of what had been taking place. They began collecting money as a gift for the family. Their goal was 50 dollars. They wound up with an amount many times their goal. My wife and I were stunned by their generosity and care. The night they took us to dinner and presented the gift will live forever in my memory. Later, I wrote a thank-you note to every person who contributed to the gift; yet that gesture could not convey my gratitude. They continue to draw from me an undying appreciation for sensitive, loving people who made our leaving better.

My family and I went on to something incredibly good. God had been the Father who cared and helped after all. In the shadows, where I could not see, He was present and active. He had worked by His schedule and on His pace, not mine. What He came up with was much better than I could have planned. I still have moments when I think about the seemingly endless experience; and I know how close I came to being pushed into the abyss. That I was not thrown over the edge was not because some folk had not tried and had not wanted badly to cheer as I dropped. I have thanked God times without number that I was not forced to "bow and scrape" in order to survive, that I was not thrown into the street. Try as I may, I cannot express my gratitude strongly enough. As I pray, I am keenly aware that some do not make it. They are the ones who are stoned by their own people. They are the wounded who are shot by their own army. They are the ones who cannot sing in a seemingly endless night. They desperately need the kind of help I received in order to survive and to continue in wholeness and hope. They are where I once was, waiting for a song in the night.

Chapter 3

Help to Walk and Not Faint

In his tremendously insightful and immensely helpful book, *Tracks of a Fellow Struggler,* John Claypool shared his prolonged, painful experience of coping with his young daughter's struggle with leukemia. In sermons to his congregation, he expressed his feelings and his faith. One of his sermons was based on Isaiah 40:31: "Those who hope in the Lord will renew their strength. They will soar on wings like eagles; they will run and not grow weary, they will walk and not be faint." He shared his discovery at what he described as the lowest point of his ordeal. In essence, Claypool stated that his agonizing experience was such that he could not soar in ecstasy or run in meaningful activity. All he could do was walk, to remain on his feet, to endure. In his helplessness, God came and gave him the power not to faint; God increased his strength to endure with patience what he could not change but had to bear.

The looming specter of my losing a pastorate or even a ministerial career cannot begin to compare with the loss of a life, with a little girl's valiant but losing struggle against leukemia. If I were fired my life and my family members' lives would go on with at least some small elements of hope and even accomplishment and enjoyment. Perhaps we would continue in a different direction, on a different economic plane, with adjusted goals and dreams and with a long struggle with bitterness; but we would go on. If the worst happened to me, I could pick up some of the pieces of a shattered career and begin the work of fitting life back together. Yet I learned in my bitter, perplexing experience of facing termination that Claypool's observation was true for me on my much lesser level. My life held fewer and fewer moments of elation. What little relief I found from pressure was always brief and overshadowed by the threat that was ever-present, pressing down on me. I found momentary relief in shared moments with family members and friends. Yet I could not soar. Like a bird with a broken wing, I fluttered along the ground and desperately longed to fly again.

I could not run. No amount of activity could solve my problem, make it easier, or force it away. I worked at my task, which had taken on dimensions of toil. I did all I knew to do in studying, preparing sermons, preaching, and ministering. I also worked hard at gaining an opportunity to move to other employment. Yet I discovered that the weariness I experienced was not as much physical as it was mental, emotional, and spiritual. The best I could do was to walk doggedly through my days. My goal was to endure, to survive.

In the crisis of threatened, impending termination, I spent a great deal of time looking for help to remain upright and moving, help to cope with each new indication of threat, help to escape. To ask for help was a drastically new departure for me; it came only with extreme effort.

Deep down in most of us, I believe, is a fierce drive or desire to be—or to be viewed as—self-sufficient. We are reluctant to admit we need help, and we often hesitate or refuse to ask for it. On one occasion, as I was working my way through seminary, my dad asked whether I needed money. I responded that I was O.K. I had enough to meet my needs. He remarked that he felt I would not admit a need for money if it existed. He had picked up on my determination to fend for myself as far as possible. Real, unrelenting pressure, however, will push aside reservations and will prompt a continuing search for, and ready acceptance of, assistance.

Where does a pastor struggling with impending forced termination find help? To what resources inside and outside himself can he turn? I began looking, and I found some sources. More are becoming available now as people in positions to help become aware of the spreading epidemic of forced pastoral terminations.

Support Group

During my long, agonizing night without song, the most effective source of ongoing help I found (actually that found me) as I endured the inky blackness of my ministerial night was a support group. Looking back, I realize I was extremely fortunate (or better, blessed). Not every pastor who is experiencing the increasing pressure of possible termination has access to a support group. Some form their own groups, meeting to encourage one another and to offer what help they can. Some may have to go to a nearby city periodically to meet with a continuing group. In my case, I almost stumbled into one of the most helpful and maturing experiences I have known. I still shudder at how close I came to missing it.

The chaplain at the largest local hospital formed a share group of five interested pastors who accepted his invitation to begin an ongoing group. I often have smiled as I recall my decision to become part of the group. When he approached me about joining, my first thought was that I really had no serious need for such a group. A second thought was that the experience might be beneficial and educational. It certainly could not hurt. Doubtless, the others in the group needed it more than I did. After all, I did not have everything under control, but at that point I was managing to hold things together most of the time. As matters turned out, no member of the group needed the support, encouragement, and help more than I did. My taking part turned out to be one of the best, most needed, and most productive actions I have taken, as a pastor and as a person.

A Caring Convener

George Cox was an incredibly gifted man. After service as a missionary to Japan he trained to become a counselor. He also developed into an accomplished artist. His insight concerning the perils and pitfalls pastors faced and his compassion for people led him to form a support group to help hurting ministers. The group met once a week for a set number of hours. George did not charge us a fee, but he did expect us to be committed enough to the group that we would set aside the time and keep the weekly appointment. Unquestionably, he was the key to what I feel was the group's success in providing support. He was openly human—sensitive, competent, insightful, and yet unyielding in his requirement that we be honest with ourselves and the group. In each session, he waited patiently for us to begin to open up and talk about a new or an ongoing difficulty or celebration. Sometimes, we were ready immediately to begin dealing with our "stuff"; at other times we waited in silence until one of us dared to lower his defenses, admit a need for help, and begin to wrestle with his feelings.

George would not allow us to disguise our real feelings by saying what we thought was expected, acceptable, or Christian. He did not let us hide behind a facade of religious language. You would think pastoral ministers would recognize readily when they were masking their real feelings out of fear that if they said what they actually felt, others would think less of them. One of the truths George helped us see was our tendency to hide our real feelings. Sometimes, we were slow to be honest with ourselves. Repeatedly, George guided us to blunt honesty about ourselves and others with whom we were dealing. He would not allow us to pretend, to protect our "images," to permit fear or embarrassment to get in the way of truth.

Everyone in the group had counseled people. We had identified masks behind which people sought to hide. We had tried to guide people to look honestly at their feelings, admit them, and work on them. Now, we had to throw off our masks and let one another see our actual faces. To do so was difficult for people who were supposed to have everything together, who ostensibly were examples or models of wholeness.

George was consistently firm. He had to be. He was in with a tough group. He would persist until he got down to where we really were living. I owe him a debt beyond my ability to pay. With his caring, no-nonsense approach, I was forced to take a good look at myself. He put me in touch with some of my strengths and weaknesses, my favorite feelings, my habitual ways of responding to people and situations, some of my hang-ups, some of the reasons for my reactions and reasoned responses, and how I viewed myself and the reasons.

George also helped me understand some of the people around me better. He helped me come to what I still feel were some reasonably accurate assessments of the reasons some of the people determined to fire me felt as they did, reasons people who went along with the continuing campaign joined the crowd, and what had touched a nerve in the church leader and had elicited such a violent reaction. I did not like these people any better, but I was beginning to understand them better. Whatever happened in the current crisis, I was learning a lot about myself and others that would stand me in good stead in the future, no matter what direction my life took.

A Shared Suffering

Pain was the common denominator in the support group. We all were hurting to some degree. Some were trying to cope with church crises. Others were working through personal problems. I was introduced to a small sample of the kinds of struggles pastors waged every day. The six of us (George also entered in by sharing some of the things he was dealing with) talked about our attempts to meet and work through the various problems we encountered. Every week, I was reminded that I was not alone in not having everything under control or not being able to keep everything together. Other people who seemed serene and complete—on top of the business of being pastors and well-integrated persons—grappled with the same or similar circumstances. I was not the only one who was unsure, hurting, and scrambling for answers. I discovered I was part of a small circle of care where acceptance was extended no matter what secrets we shared—some for the first time as we were forced to look honestly at ourselves. To bring out into the open for the first time feelings we barely admitted to ourselves, to wait for response, and to receive acceptance was healing. Not once that I can recall was an honest expression rejected, though plenty of not-quite-honest statements were. Hurting made us brothers on a deeper level than any other mutual factors could have done. We became comrades in crisis but also in compassion.

A Transforming Truth

One of the most important truths to which George introduced me was my need to assume responsibility for myself. What did I want? How could I get to where I wanted to be? What resources were available to help me get there?

I am an only child. For longer than normal, I had been dependent on my parents to a great degree. They took care of me. I had assumed—and wanted—the church to take care of me in the sense of offering a secure environment in which to live and work. I even had assumed that God always would take care of me; He would fix things for me. For the first time, in clear and unmistakable terms, George guided me to the truth that to a great extent, I must take care of me and those in my care. Later, a pastor-counselor drove home the truth that God will not fix for me what I can fix but refuse to do so.

A cardinal rule in writing is to write in a manner that ensures you will not be misunderstood. I do not wish to be misunderstood at this point. To trust totally in my few, weak skills would be idolatry. Because of my crisis and support-group experience, my faith in God has deepened. I depend on Him; I trust Him to help me in His way according to His timetable. Yet I strongly believe He steadfastly refuses to do for me what I can do for myself. I no longer can say casually and easily that God will take care of things, that He will provide, or that He will fix things if I wait patiently. I have to be busy doing all I know to do and am able to do with the firm conviction that God is at the outer limits of my abilities. I must use all the resources available to me—internal and external, including caring people—while I pray that God will work through my efforts and through people.

I am convinced that as we work to assume responsibility for ourselves, God is in the whole process, working with us to help us grow. He works with and through our intelligence, skills, and personalities as we remain open to Him. When we come to the ends of our ropes, God stands with outstretched hand to take up where our strength and resources leave off.

Normally, I am not an actively aggressive person; I am passively aggressive. However, armed with the clear truth that I must assume responsibility for myself, I began to take every initiative to gain an opportunity for freedom. I swallowed huge chunks of pride and asked for help. I began to review my gifts and skills. I tried to broaden my alternatives where occupation was concerned. I was willing to go to another pastorate, to teach, or to assume a denominational role. Interestingly, in retrospect, I did not seriously consider secular work, although if forced, I was open to that option. For one thing, I was not trained for that area of vocation. Yet overriding that element was a desire to continue in my calling. I never put the thought into words, but I now feel that the concern was to continue in a ministry-oriented role, to continue in the direction I began years ago. George, my chaplain friend, helped me and the other group members look at all available possibilities and to refuse to limit our alternatives.

Grace for Grief

Church-related difficulties were not the only items on the support group's weekly agendas. Members related personal problems, and we were helped as persons as well as pastors. Family problems, financial needs, and personal development claimed attention.

All group members continued to struggle to see ourselves honestly and to begin to work on ourselves. As far as we could, we shared one member's continuing grief over the death of his wife and his task of rearing a son alone. Some of us were grappling with the deaths of significant people. Others were dealing with the deaths of ideals and dreams about the pastoral ministry. The emergence of harsh realities involved in church-related work generated pain and grief.

The darkness of my night without song was deepened by my mother's death. She had suffered heart problems for a number of years, and a heart attack took her life. Her death was sudden, and I was unprepared. I went through the same grief process I had witnessed others experience and with which I had attempted to help them. I knew the stages of grief and recognized all along the way what was happening in me. Such understanding helped, but it did not make grief any easier to bear.

I decided not to dominate a support-group session with my grief. Underneath that decision likely lay an aversion to talking through a painful experience that would result in a display of emotion. I would grieve alone. When I did not bring up the subject, however, one of the group members did. George gently and kindly encouraged me to talk about my feelings, and the group members shared in a grief that some of them had worked through. Such sharing helped me enter into others' grief as they later invited the group to sit and weep with them.

One of the most moving group sessions in which I participated was one in which a man who still is a good and valued friend expressed his grief over being ousted as pastor of his church. He wept openly at what was happening to him and his family. He wept out of helplessness and anger, but he also wept out of grief over something good that had died. He had given himself extensively in ministering to church members' needs, but suddenly his services no longer were wanted. His work ended abruptly, and in that occurrence his image of the church had been shattered. As Job of old had done, my friend was sitting on the trash heap of a broken dream. Unlike Job's erstwhile friends, the group had no easy theological answers. and certainly made no thoughtless accusations or gave advice as they had done. Had we attempted to offer advice and answers, George would have intervened. We entered into our brother's grief as far as we could. We sat with him on his trash heap, and some of us did so with the raw, chilling realization that any one of us could be next.

Grief that is shared is not dissipated totally. It may not even become lighter or less severe. It does become more manageable, more bearable, because of people who listen with genuine care.

Sound Suggestions

George never gave the group members advice. He made suggestions that we could weigh for ourselves. To this day, I have followed his lead in counseling. I do not give advice. I am not smart enough or experienced enough to give good, foolproof advice. Besides, what works for one person may not work for someone else. As George was fond of pointing out, when you give advice two things can happen, and one of them is devastatingly negative. If the advice works, the advice-giver looks like a genius and earns the gratitude of the person advised. If the advice does not work, the person advised becomes angry, accuses the advisor of incompetence, and spreads the word about a counselor who does not know what he is talking about.

On the day of the infamous meeting I have called "The Great Deacons' Meeting," I called George, made an appointment with him, and went to his office. He had invited the support group members to call him if crises arose, and I took him up on the gracious offer. In our lengthy conversation, I explained what was happening and listened to his suggestion about possible responses. What he said made sense to me; I could avoid taking an adversarial position and becoming defensive by how I responded to accusations or charges. A great part of the reason the meeting went as well for me as it did was George's shared insights concerning a situation in which a pastor was outnumbered badly and needed to buy some time. I remain in his debt.

Family

Throughout my long and excruciating ordeal, my family's love and support helped me remain determined to walk on. My wife's love, affirmation, and encouragement were steady sources of strength for determined endurance. She stood with me. She took more than her share of blows, and she hurt when I took mine. She did her best to bolster my sagging ego and to provide a home setting that was a haven from the storm whose intensity grew steadily. She struggled, as I did, with the harshness and coldness we encountered; but her inner strength and tenacity helped keep both of us going.

Our children were small, and they could not grasp the full impact of what was happening except to pick up on our emotions that were strong and always near the surface. I hurt for them because through no fault of their own they were caught up in the storm raging around them. They never will know how much they helped me, there in the darkness. They loved me unconditionally. Their spontaneous affection and delightful expressions of discovery as they soaked up life brought fresh air and fragrance to my world's stifling atmosphere.

My time with my children was one of the few genuine sources of joy and laughter I experienced. To them, I was a significant person. I was not a pastor; I was their father who loved them dearly. My children's laughter, enchantment with life, and sense of wonder brought warmth and hope to an otherwise senseless, mindless circumstance.

My in-laws and my parents were active in their churches. They never had witnessed up close the kind of struggle my wife and I were enduring. They were puzzled and deeply troubled by what was happening to us. What they did that was most helpful was assure us they were with us. My wife's parents were extremely open and sympathetic in volunteering their resources if we were summarily ousted.

I came to a new and stronger appreciation for my family, for the bonds that remained strong through terrific stresses and strains. I shudder to think what could have happened to me—and within me—if I had not had the constant love and support of a loyal family.

Friends

The farther I had moved through life, the more I had come to value friendships with people who had invited me across their defensive space into their lives to share them. In my darkness, some hands reached out to touch, to support, and to affirm. One pastor friend worked hard and consistently to gain opportunities for me to move. Others listened; they literally came and stood with me. They expressed care and offered all the support they could give.

George, my chaplain friend, led support members to see that every pastor needs a friend who has a vocation other than religious and who is outside the pastor's congregation. Such a friend can be objective, and that person can be an invaluable sounding-board for a pastor's feelings, problems, and frustrations. I did not realize at the time that George was that person for me. He was not in my church, and he was not in a totally "religious vocation." He brought badly needed objectivity to my crisis.

Dogged Faith

I wish I could state that during my long night without song, my faith never wavered. I would like to say that my trust in God and my confidence that He would help me work things out remained strong and constant. I cannot do so. My faith reached lows as well as highs, and I found I was not alone in experiencing fluctuating faith.

An older member of my congregation, who was a friend and supporter, had a son who was pastor of a church in another city in our state. He was going through the same kind of crisis experience I faced. One night, after evening worship, I asked her how her son was doing. Things were not going well, she answered. As tears formed in her eyes, she asked me to pray for him. Then she said with courageous honesty that the pressure to which he was being subjected was affecting her faith. She did not need to explain further. I knew too well what she meant.

What I had was a stubborn faith that held on tight to the belief that the God whom I had known and worshiped most of my life—the God who had been so near on the night of joyous song many years ago—is just, merciful, and caring. Through doubt, anger, and uncertainty, I still talked with Him. I doggedly held on to the truth that I was His child, and that while I expected no favoritism from Him, He had to be more than One who stood idly by in the face of injustice. He had to be standing in the shadows, watching over His own.

Later, when the darkness finally lifted, I thanked God quickly and often. Gratitude took and still retains a larger place in my relationship with Him. I do not know the reason I survived—rather, received a wider opportunity. I was not and am not God's favored child; I am no better or more deserving than countless others who have endured and are enduring similar experiences. I only know my faith has been strengthened in the God who works in His way and on His timetable.

Little Things

During my trek through darkness, perhaps for the first time I literally began to take life one day at a time. I believed deeply and had preached that life is lived most meaningfully when we try to use each day to the full, when we accept each day as a gift from God and try to be good stewards of that day. Now, I began to try to live one day at a time, through necessity. Sometimes, I merely wanted to move through the day safely; and I counted every day I survived as a victory. Often, I had prayed for God's light for my next step; now I concentrated on that next step.

I focused on continuing to do my work well. Many times, mentally and emotionally exhausted, I forced myself to make a good effort. Involved were personal integrity and a sense of responsibility to God, my calling, some good people, and myself. In addition, because I felt that some church members were looking for any ammunition they could find to use against me. I was determined to head off any charge of dereliction of duty.

I began to relish little things again. Spoken or written words of encouragement, timely words of appreciation, a good book, inspiring music, the feeling of something done well under adverse circumstances—these and other seemingly small things helped me make my way through my days. Every now and then, someone who counted would express his or her feeling that what was happening to me and my family was not right. Some persons outside the church expressed understanding of, and disgust for, what was taking place.

A neighboring rural church helped me more than the members ever will know. I was invited to preach a revival there. Then, several times I was invited back to speak. The people's warmth, acceptance, and open affirmation contrasted sharply to my own church situation. That small, caring congregation became an oasis, a place of refuge and renewal for me. My love and appreciation for those people will continue through my remaining years. My denomination's leaders can talk all they wish about the "great" super churches. I know a truly great church, small in size but huge in spirit, whose members ministered to me in my pain when I needed it most.

In my ordeal, I was forced to look to small things for comfort and encouragement, and I rediscovered that they have a power all out of proportion to their degree or dimensions. I try not to forget that truth.

New Incentive

In my long night's journey toward day and renewed song, I received help to walk and not faint. Some caring, compassionate people gave of their time, energy, and love. As far as they could they shared my struggle. In God's providence, one the things I want most is to offer that kind of help to beleaguered pastors whose "sun [has] set while it is still day" (Jer. 15:9).

Chapter 4

Causes of Crisis

"Help! I *need* your help! On Tuesday our church's deacons asked me to resign, and it appears that I will have no choice in the matter." These were the opening words of a letter I received from a pastor in another state. After my move from the pastorate to a new opportunity, I had spoken in his church in my city, and we had become friends. He had moved to a different pastorate. After years of ministry, he encountered difficulty. The deacons had set a termination date, but the friend was trying to negotiate a different date to "buy some time." As I read the words, I felt the old stirrings in the pit of my stomach. Another pastor was faced with being terminated, and he had to find a place to go as quickly as possible. He had joined the swiftly swelling ranks of a vast number of pressured, harried victims.

Sometime later, I received a letter from another pastor friend in one of our southern states. He had been a member of the last church I served as pastor. He was contacting his friends to make them aware of his situation. Under pressure, he had agreed to resign his church but had negotiated a "grace period." He would be given time to find an opportunity to move. In the letter my friend asked that I be on the look-out for a church that might be interested in him. Still later, I received a second letter from him. No opportunity had arisen for him to relocate. He had talked with several search committees, but nothing had developed. He was letting friends know he had resigned his church rather than create a situation in which he might win a vote to remain but see the church become divided or actually split. He was upbeat and hopeful. He wrote that he felt God was leading him out of the pastoral ministry to some other role of ministry, and he was taking steps to determine that new ministry.

A friend from seminary days had visited me at my place of work. He and I had been exchanging pleasantries and catching up on each other's news. I walked with him to the elevator that would take him down to the first floor of our building and turned to go back to my office. I heard him say, "They're dropping around me like flies." I stopped, turned, and stepped back toward him. "The pastors around me are dropping like flies." He went on to say that a pastor near him had been forced to resign. My friend said that at the moment, he was secure.

I sat in the home's living room talking with a man who had been a seminary acquaintance. As a part-time staff member of my church, I was visiting him to invite his family and him to visit our church. I had known him, but not well. I had not seen him for years, and the last I had known of him, he was a "successful" pastor. Now, he was with an insurance company. As we talked and sort of caught up on each other's activities since our seminary years, he made an interesting and revealing statement on which he did not elaborate. He did not need to do so. In essence, he said: "I don't ever want to be dependent on a church again for my livelihood." I knew immediately what he meant, and I guessed that the deep feelings behind the statement were generated by the memory of a painful experience in his pastoral ministry.

A coworker asked whether I knew a certain pastor in another state. I recognized the name and replied that I had met him years ago when we were pastors in the same area. My coworker said the pastor needed to find another church. A group of men in his church had decided he had been at the church long enough. They determined the time had come for him to move on. So, without warning and in the name of the Lord, they were sending the pastor packing.

Among the men I know who have moved from the pastoral ministry to other vocations or other spheres of service, the dominant feeling about their moves is relief, a sense of release and freedom. Why is this true? Certainly the unique, varied, and unrelenting pressures of the pastorate form part of the explanation. In addition, the petty, trivial demands and irritations that nibble away at a pastor play their parts. Yet I think a major component of the sense of release comes from a feeling of a more secure niche or stance than is possible in the pastoral ministry. The feeling is one of being freed from a sometimes overwhelming number of people who have a disproportionate amount of input into, and even control over, the pastor and his family.

The termination of pastors—ministerial firings—is a mushrooming problem that spans denominations. The firings are growing at an alarming rate. The pastors who attend conferences and seminars that deal with termination and its aftershocks represent the tip of the iceberg. Many pastors who see the handwriting on their study walls are seeking help in heading off the kind of confrontation that ends with their terminations. Others are in denial, reluctant to admit a crisis exists. Still others struggle in lonely isolation; they have no source of help or do not know where to seek it. Many are caught completely by surprise when the demand for their termination is presented to them or to their churches.

Forced termination of pastors is not confined to a few isolated incidents. It now is an increasingly accepted way to effect pastoral changes. It is widespread and alarmingly frequent. What are some of the causes of this growing epidemic? I am convinced that the causes are many; but I also am fairly certain that if the dominant group in a congregation—and in some cases, one powerful person—wants to get rid of a pastor, almost any reason, real or imagined, is enough. Clearly defined causes of termination, however have surfaced.

In the Introduction, I referred to statistics supplied by LifeWay Christian Resources of the Southern Baptist Convention. Included in the materials were causes of forced termination: lack of unity and the presence of factions in the church, conflict over leadership styles, relational incompetence, and tenure. Primary reasons included lack of communication, problems related to immorality and unethical conduct, performance dissatisfaction, authoritarian leadership style, power struggles, and personality conflicts. In the 1999 survey, the most common causes for terminations "cited by directors of missions in reports to state convention church-minister relations directors were: control issues regarding who will run the church; poor people skills of the pastor, pastoral leadership style perceived as too strong, the church's resistance to change, and the [church's already being] conflicted when the pastor arrived."[5] Perhaps the study's most startling statistic was that only 55 percent of pastors who experienced forced termination returned to church-related vocations; 45 percent did not do so.

Clearly, both churches and pastors provide causes for forced terminations. I believe churches contribute at least five major causes:

1. One of the primary causes of forced termination is what I have termed "lighting up the scoreboard." We live in a statistics-oriented society. Most often, in many areas, results are tabulated "by the numbers." Businesses, professional and amateur athletics, and churches want leaders who can produce glowing numbers. By and large, churches have adopted the profit-and-loss approach, or the success syndrome: The ledger must show a positive result when the minuses and the pluses are tabulated each year. The yardstick for a pastor's ministry can be made up of number of baptisms recorded, number of members gained (whether or not the church is in a growth-area), building programs launched and/or completed, and size of budget met. Generally, I feel, churches have adopted our society's executive-corporation model: They want a chairman of the board who can make their company show ever-increasing profits. Often, the methods employed to do this are acceptable as long as they work. The question being asked by some church power structures is not, "Is it sound practice?" The question is," Does it work?" If something is effective in attracting people to the church and increasing the church roll and monetary gifts, it must be "blessed of God."

I often have said that the parallels between churches and athletic teams in our society are startling. The parallels between pastors and coaches/managers seem evident. If the team is winning, the manager or the coach is a great guy, a genius who makes all the right moves. If the team is losing, the coach or manager is replaced. The idea is that the team is alright; the coach or manager is at fault and must be replaced. Seldom, I think, do congregations look at themselves and conclude they are lax in

---

[5] LifeWay Christian Resources website.

attending, visiting, giving, or developing warmth and openness of fellowship. If a church does not attain a perceived level of success, the pastor must be at fault.

I do not subscribe to a convention speaker's dogmatic declaration that if anything is wrong with a church's direction, ministry, or growth, the fault lies with the pastor. In a percentage of cases, the pastor is at fault. Yet a church may decide not to follow a pastor's lead; the members may not want to add new people who might threaten members' tightly held positions; the congregation may not want prophetic preaching that is challenging and disturbing. Sometimes, a pastor does all he knows to do to motivate members to engage in outreach, ministry, and fellowship, only to see his efforts ignored or resisted. In some cases, he discovers that the church expects his staff (if the church has one) and him to do all the work because they were hired to do so.

A letter to The Baptist Program magazine summed up well the "hired hand" perception of the pastoral ministry: "Many churches 'hire' a preacher rather than accept his divine call to that place of ministry. Consequently, they say, 'We hired him, we can fire him.'"[6] We live in a society of hiring and firing, and this mind-set has been brought into the pastor-church relationship. What often is being left out is the element of divine leading or calling. On the front end, when the pastor is called to a church, the element of God's will is prominent. On the back end, when the pastor is fired, this element seldom, if ever, is mentioned.

2. A second causal element churches contribute to pastoral firings is what I have sensed to be a growing lack of respect for the pastoral role or position. Comparing my recollections of how people in general viewed pastors during my growing-up years in a small Mississippi town with present prevailing views, I have detected a change in people's attitude toward the pastoral role. If pastors ever were given automatic authority when they moved to churches, they no longer receive that gift. Their churches will decide whether they will allow pastors to lead. In addition, pastors do not receive automatic respect. True to the attitude prevalent in

---

[6] *The Baptist Program,* October, 1981, p. 23.

our society as a whole, churches' attitude seems to be "wait-and-see." Pastors and their families may or may not be accepted by a congregation or a community. My best guess is that a large number of church folk do not have a significantly high regard for the pastoral role. Some if not many of them view the pastor as living off the good graces of his church.

In an interview for a seminary's theological journal, James T. Draper, Jr., then president of the Southern Baptist Convention, said he had noticed a disturbing change among Southern Baptist churches. It was "an increasing disregard for ministers that is recent. I don't mean that a pastor should be a Pope or a dictator. But there is a lack of respect which is evidenced by the dismissal of pastors and staff members, which has become an epidemic in Southern Baptist life."[7]

Of course, in a real sense pastors must earn respect by their commitment, integrity, spiritual depth, genuine care, and the way they do their work. A pastor friend worked extra hard and longer days than normal during the first years of his pastorate to restore respect and trust a former pastor had destroyed through laziness and carelessness. Pastors must deserve their people's respect. On the other hand, their role is a divine calling; they and their congregations must treat it as such. Lack of respect for the pastoral role can lead to the easy dismissal of pastors.

3. A third contribution churches make to pastoral terminations is their gauging a pastor's effectiveness in terms of the pastor's age. In our youth-obsessed society, age has become a factor in pastoral firings. Many churches want a young pastor to give the congregation an image of energy and vitality. These churches want to appeal to youth, singles, and young couples. They often are willing to overlook inexperience and lack of skills in some areas if a pastor's youthful appearance and exuberance come across as attractive from the pulpit, are expressed in vibrant personality, and are effective in relating to the congregation's cross section of members.

---

[7] *The Theological Educator,* Number 28, Spring, 1984, p. 14.

Many times, what becomes lost easily in the quest for youth at the helm is the accumulated wisdom, experience, insight, and sensitivity of a pastor who is over fifty and has come to terms with aging. Granted, this is not always the case; number of years does not necessarily translate into wisdom, and all pastors do not benefit from their experiences. Yet in many cases, in the areas of preaching content, caring, and counseling, older pastors have a great deal to offer.

In our society, aging is a specter we grudgingly accept. The truth, however, is that more people are living longer; gray is becoming an increasingly prominent color. One area in which pastors must offer help, by example and word, is in the aging process in an age denying-time. Out of dealing with this fact of life themselves, pastors can assist people in coming to terms with the aging process. In a disposable, throw-away society, we cannot afford to consign pastors to the scrap heap because they no longer are young. If we do, we senselessly are throwing away one of our most valuable resources.

One of the most amazing pastors I have known was well into his 60's, if not past 70, when I first met him. He was pastor of a small church in the association; but in reality, he was the whole area's pastor. Most people knew him, and many stopped him on his rounds to talk—and, I suspect, to receive a little of his boundless care. He and his wife ministered to some elderly people in a government housing project in the area. Seldom have I known a man who worked as hard, though maybe not as fast, and who was more admired, respected, and loved than he was. We who knew and observed him would have been much poorer had we not shared his freely given wealth of wisdom.

Largely, in my denomination opportunities to continue a pastoral ministry diminish rapidly with and following middle-age. One pastor expressed his fear and apprehension that aging brings to numerous pastors. He wrote, "After twenty years in the ministry I'm sitting on a church time bomb...and it's rough....Where can an old boy fifty-four years old find another pastorate?"[8] At age 54, a

---

[8] *The Baptist Program,* September, 1981, p. 20.

pastor should have many productive years left; yet my perception is that Southern Baptist churches looking for or willing to accept pastors over 50 are relatively few. Another person wrote: "A friend in his mid-fifties has been asked to leave his pastorate of a dozen years. He asks, 'Where do they expect me to go? I have been trying to get out for the past five years. No church will have me because of my age.' "[9] The tragedy of this truth is etched deeply into the faces of men who are fired because they no longer are young.

    4. A fourth element churches sometimes bring to pastoral terminations is a preconceived notion concerning a pastor's tenure. In their view, their pastors "overstay their welcome," as people in my native state used to say. Much has been said and written about the relatively short average tenures of Southern Baptist pastors. Although average tenures have increased over time, they still are fairly brief. What has not been pointed out in the implication that, as a whole, pastors are prone to move frequently is that some churches do not want or expect long pastorates.

    If the reasons for the "short tenure" expectation of some churches could be determined, the delineation would be interesting. My hunch is that at least three factors are involved in this mind-set: (1) For pastors to live in communities and to work with a congregation for an extended period of time would mean they would learn a great deal about most of the people, and this could be threatening to some of them. (2) The longer pastors stay, the greater the possibility is that they will gather more authority for themselves or shift the church's power base to different people. This poses a threat to the existing power structure. (3) Some churches like change for variety's sake; they like the parade of new personalities, ideas, and approaches.

    Sometimes, when a pastor stays beyond an invisible time line, some in the congregation begin getting restless. A pastor who was being fired in a coup led by several men in the church had committed the serious sin of staying too long. The only reason given for ousting him was that the time had come for him to go.

---

[9] Ibid., p. 23.

The self-appointed instruments of God's will to swell the ranks of the ministerial unemployed begin to ask questions: "When is the pastor ever going to move?" "What if no other church becomes interested?" "The pastor has been here long enough; don't you think?" "Don't you think the church would do better with new pastoral leadership?" A pastor's wife wrote of her and her husband's shock when he suddenly was terminated: "We were involved in 'Let's run the preacher off'....it really was a surprise. We came back from vacation and really thought the people loved us, they treated us so nice. But, as one man told my husband, two years is long enough for any preacher to stay at a church."[10] Granted, some pastors may have a two-or three-year "program" they implement; and when that program or file of sermons is done, they are ready to move on. The other side of the coin is that churches may have their time schedules for their pastors.

What is extremely difficult for serious pastors and sensitive churches in the matter of tenure often is: When is the right time to go? The wife of a pastor who had been given a deadline of termination told my wife, in essence: "We had chances to leave before now. But my husband and I prayed about it, and we felt that the Lord was leading us to stay." Where is the Lord's leading in the matter of pastoral tenure? If He is the One who indicates to pastors and churches when a tenure of service is over, how is His will found and implemented? What if some church members think the pastor should go, but the pastor feels God wants him to stay? To me, the tragedy is that too often in pastoral terminations, God's guidance is not considered or at least conveniently is confused with personal opinions and preferences.

In the years following my close brush with forced termination, in one church I witnessed up close two sad spectacles of pastors' being given deadlines that would mark the end of their tenures. In both instances, as a member of the church, I had the opportunity to speak on behalf of both men. Looking back, I regret not saying more and not speaking more forcefully.

---

[10] *The Baptist Program*, October, 1981, p, 13.

The first pastor was in his late 50's and had served the church for more than 20 years. Some members felt the church had outgrown him; he had overstayed his time and no longer was in step with the church, they indicated. In a fairly heated meeting, he was given a deadline. He tried to move, but nothing developed. When the deadline arrived, he was terminated. One of his long-time friends had set up a fund to which members could give voluntarily. This allowed the pastor to continue a retirement program he had started years before. As matters developed, members loyal to him made substantial provision. Still, he was fired at an age that made finding another pastorate extremely difficult. In the whole process of his termination, one glaring omission stood out to me: Not once was the indication given that this was God's will or God's clear signal to anybody. A vocal and adamant segment of the congregation made the determination. In the aftermath, nothing could be done to correct or to make up for the damage inflicted on the pastor and his family—or on the church's image and reputation.

The second pastor was in his early-to-mid 50's and had served the church for about six years. As in the previous case of termination, a vocal segment in the congregation pressed for the pastor to be removed. Others in the church were opposed to a quick, forced termination. The church opted to engage a mediator to help resolve the conflict. The resulting recommendation was that the pastor resign immediately and receive a severance package consisting of several months' pay at a rate less than his current salary. The pastor and his wife were devastated. He knew he could not remain and be effective. He would continue the efforts he had begun to relocate. He knew, and I had pointed out in the meeting in which the mediation report was presented, that the mills of Southern Baptist pastor selection grind exceeding slow. In addition, forced termination on a resume was a distinct disadvantage. Four years after he was fired, he received an invitation to resume his pastoral ministry. If his experience mirrors my close brush with pastoral death, my guess is that he and his family will still spend some time dealing with anger and bitterness. They will bear the livid scars of their experience.

Whether or not the people involved in the church's two forced terminations realized it, the damage inflicted on the church will remain as a dark shadow on its history. To me, the tragedy remains that both situations could have been handled differently. Calmer and more insightful, compassionate negotiations could have resulted in transitions that would have been much less painful and disruptive—and even would have been redemptive.

5. A fifth factor churches contribute to pastoral terminations is members' becoming enamored with mega-church pastors and comparing them with their own pastors. Members of smaller congregations may view the pastor-celebrities on television or hear them at conventions and other meetings and may expect their pastors to be as "dynamic" as the ecclesiastical stars. In one of my friend's letters to which I referred earlier, the deacons' primary reason for asking him to resign was that he was not offering "dynamic leadership" for the church. Of course, all pastors do not have equal skills, and many do not remotely want to imitate the superstars. These pastors want to use their abilities in ways that are their own styles. To some church members, these pastors may pale in comparison with the denominational celebrities.

In addition, church members can become staunch fans of the attractive figures who have their own television productions and book and tape ministries. A minister of education invited me to lead a Bible study in his church. I met and had opportunity to talk with the church's pastor. During one conversation, he related an incident in which, after a worship service, a church member confronted him. The member charged that the pastor's interpretation of a certain Scripture passage did not agree with the interpretation of an acclaimed television preacher, the pastor of a mega-church in the state. The clear implication was that the local pastor's interpretation had to be wrong because the super-pastor certainly was right.

Only a few pastors attain celebrity status. Some churches revel in their pastors' stardom; others would like to attract highly visible leaders. Most pastors, however, will labor in relative obscurity. When they are compared with and measured by the larger-than-life images of the few who have attained star status, they come off something worse than second-best. The tendency may be to replace the pastors with flamboyant, dramatic, take-charge stars on the rise.

The subtle difficulty the pastoral-celebrity image presents provides an appropriate segue into elements pastors contribute to terminations. Sadly, pastors can set in motion the process that leads to their firings; they can suffer the pain of self-inflicted wounds that result in their demise.

1. The "super-pastor" image is trumpeted widely in the religious and secular media. A number of pastors with great communication skills, stage presence, and forceful personalities are held up as the standard for pastoral leadership. A quick scan of conference- and convention-speaker lineups will reveal indications of who the pastoral models are. Most often, these are the dynamic and often autocratic leaders, many of whom are seen by large television audiences.

The danger of the super-pastor model is that some fledgling or even experienced pastors may try to imitate that model and to implement super-church programs in churches that cannot fund or staff them, or are not in the least interested in them. (This is the flip side of the coin mentioned previously.) Most pastors are in relatively small churches, many with limited resources and personnel.

Some churches may want autocratic leadership. They want a pastor who "calls the shots." Some professional people make decisions and give directives all week and want a pastor who does that for them in their church. I smile as I look back at the churches I served as pastor. I never entertained the thought of accumulating the power of full control. I remember deacon bodies who would have run me out of Dodge before sundown. They would have rented the U-Haul, helped me load it, and given me a map with the easiest and fastest way out of town clearly marked. My guess is that some surprised pastors have attempted to assume control in their churches and quickly lost their pastorates.

Some pastors have tried to implement big programs in small churches. Years ago, I sat in a crowd of pastors at a state convention while one of the leading pastors of the time told us what his mega-church was doing and how the church was doing it. What he said did not remotely apply to most of us; we needed ideas for what we could do in our small churches and average situations. So, ambitious pastors on their way to making their marks may expect too much from their congregations. The result well may be growing tension between the pastors and their churches.

2. A second factor pastors sometimes provide in forced terminations is their failure to do the work. Sometimes, for whatever reasons, pastors cannot do efficiently the tasks their churches want and need performed. They simply do not have the skills or tools. The job is too big, too complex, too demanding. They are overmatched. They are not prepared properly to handle the situation. The churches made a mistake in gauging the pastors' abilities; the pastors made a mistake by jumping in over their heads, perhaps misreading God's leading. This is one situation in which love and patience will move a congregation to negotiate with the pastor to allow him time and to give him help in finding his niche. To misunderstand or to misinterpret God's will in this area is not the foremost mistake for a congregation or a pastor; for a church and/or pastor to fail to deal with it in honesty and fairness is a far greater error.

Pastors' willful refusal to do their jobs is inexcusable and is legitimate grounds for action by their congregations. My interaction with pastor-search committees sometimes were frustrating, but they also were educational. In outlining what they expected of a pastor, they often revealed difficulties with previous pastors. Some pastors had purposely and willfully evaded their duties. Some had made themselves inaccessible to members, taking frequent and unannounced trips, playing golf or fishing too frequently, or barricading themselves in their studies. After I became a layman, a pastor of my church gave partial attention and energy to the church while he established a business on the side, though the church paid him adequately. Let me be clear: The emphasis here is on actual dereliction of duty, not on imagined failings or unfounded supposition.

I do not mean that because the pastor did not anticipate needs without being informed of them, or was not in the office when someone called at a reasonable hour, or did not know about a member in the hospital, the pastor was guilty of laziness or lack of care. Yet if pastors become stale because of a lack of reading, studying, or working at improving pastoral skills, they cheat themselves and their people. If pastors do not seek opportunities to grow personally and professionally, to deepen personal spirituality, to work at relational and caring skills, they have chosen mediocrity.

In the course of my pastoral ministry, I became interested in western novels for my recreational reading. I ran across the opinion that Owen Wister's novel *The Virginian* gave rise to the genre. As I read the book, I came across an exchange between two characters that became a continuing challenge for me as a pastor. One of the characters offered emphatically: "I'll tell yu' this: a middlin' doctor is a pore thing, and a middlin' lawyer is a pore thing; but keep me from a middlin' man of God."[11] No pastor should settle for being a "middlin' man of God."

A good friend of mine, a pastor I respect deeply, feels keenly his responsibility to provide care for his congregation. To be with his church members in their crises and to attempt to meet their needs is a vital part of his role; to do so is not an imposition or an "extra." Also, his "being there" has forged a strong bond between him and a large part of his congregation. He has built a high degree of credibility with his people by giving his best effort consistently.

Serious pastors must do their work—in preaching, teaching, visiting, administering, counseling, and caring. To earn and wear the label *lazy* is to merit a congregation's ire if not contempt. This is not to suggest that pastors have no time off; they must have time to relax, pursue hobbies, enjoy recreation, and do advanced study. They must have times and places to "recharge their batteries." Yet pastors who do not hustle, who do not work at discharging their God-called responsibilities, are poor representatives of the Christ who never has called anyone to mediocrity. Though I am convinced pastors who do not work or who do their work casually or halfheartedly comprise a vast minority, those in this category do

---

[11] Owen Wister, *The Virginian: A Horseman of the Plains*, p. 158.

invite the moves of their congregations to secure other, more energetic pastoral ministry.

3. A third element that sometimes enters the mix resulting in pastoral termination is a pastor's lack of tending staff relationships. Often, the result is conflict with staff members. This is especially crucial when conflict occurs between the pastor and a staff member who has preceded the pastor and has built up a following in the congregation. Any conflict with the staff member is bound to alienate the pastor from the staff member's friends, especially if the pastor has not had time to establish his/her credibility, integrity, and openness to relate. Staff relationships are highly important for the church's sound ministry. Also, if trouble develops, the pastor can be labeled as hard to work with or to relate to. "We need a pastor who can get along with a staff" can be a prelude to dismissal, or at least can be one more nail driven into the coffin.

4. A pastor's knowingly or unknowingly crossing a church's power structure—or failing to observe a power structure exists, who comprises it, and how it operates—can cause the pastoral sun to begin setting while it is yet day. The ministerial music can begin to die quickly. Sometimes, a pastor realizes this crucial, and often fatal, mistake only after the fact.

The scene still is sharp and clear in my memory. At some point after my long night of living with constant threat began—about the middle, as I recall—I was visiting in the home of a church family. The wife was extremely active in the church; her husband was inconsistent in his involvement. He was personable, and I liked him. During the conversation, he touched on my troubled situation. The essence of our conversation was revealing. He asked whether I knew what my first crucial mistake was as pastor, the mistake that put me crosswise with influential people in the church. I responded that I had made so many mistakes, I had no idea what the first one was, and I was only half-kidding.

The man asked whether I remembered the day several years previously when a certain church member came to my office. I recalled the incident clearly. The visitor approached me with the proposal that the church establish a private school in the church's facilities. The city's public school system had been paired with an adjoining all-black city's school. White elementary school children would begin attending the formerly all-black school. The man in my office did not want his children and other church families' children to attend school in the black community. He wanted me to recommend to the church that we begin a new school. I declined to lead the church to establish a school. The man responded that he would take his tithe elsewhere and left my office in a huff.

The man in whose home I was visiting suggested that my response to the new-school proposal was my first big mistake. He said that my visitor was not speaking merely for himself but was a messenger for others in the church, some of whom he named, who used the semi-active church member as a spokesman. My mistake was not going along with the suggestion.

Immediately, the truth dawned on me, albeit a little late. The people my conversationalist named were part of the church's power structure, one of whom also had mentioned the possibility of a private school in the church. Another was a person whom numerous others watched in order to get a signal concerning how he stood on matters. No wonder I was getting no support from some people who could make a difference in my circumstance! Likely, they were hoping for, if not actively working for, what to them would be my timely demise. They probably were only too happy to have me under constant pressure, though they could not afford to take part openly.

Economic factors dictated that some church members who wanted me gone had to be careful. They could not be vocal openly in calling for my termination. To do so would be to risk losing clients or customers. Besides, in their view I was temporary, transient, merely passing through. Thus, I was expendable. I had not played ball with the right people, and I would be removed from the game. I had crossed the power structure.

5. Another factor pastors can contribute to their dismissals is making unguarded comments to trusted church members about other members, even if the comments are valid. No matter how accurate the observations may be, they can be used as deadly weapons at the precise moment when they can do the most

damage to the pastor. The people who relay the pastor's conversations may have concurred with the statements, may have broached the subject, or may have made similar of stronger statements. Yet what is relayed in the heat of battle is what the pastor said negatively, and what was said in unguarded moments may prove to be fatal.

I victimized myself in the area of unguarded statements. No one ever came to me to confront me with something I had said—or allegedly said—that was critical of that person. Yet I had the gut-level feeling that at least one key family in the whole painful episode had been told of careless words I had said. I take full responsibility for having been so insensitive and unwise. I learned from my mistake, almost in the wreckage of pastoral crisis that the unwise remarks helped create.

6. Some pastors' confessional preaching and approach may present a difficulty for congregations who put their pastors "on a pedestal." Some church members still cling to the belief that their pastor has the answers, has conquered all doubts, has risen above the members of the congregation in spiritual attainment. For pastors to confess that they wrestle with some difficulties, do not have all the theological answers, are not sure how God thinks and acts in every situation, and has some spiritual maturing to do upsets—and even threatens—them. They do not want a pastor who is learning and growing with them but one who has arrived and is flawless. Sometimes, when a pastor openly confesses to be human like his church members, some hearers use what they view as a decided weakness to hasten the pastor's departure. Pastors need to understand the risks involved in confessional preaching; accepting that risk and proceeding with courage is rewarding but also may be costly.

Often, in mutual dynamics or tensions, both pastors and churches contribute elements that lead to pastoral terminations. I have identified two mutual factors I believe are especially significant.

1. Conflicting personalities can lead to a pastor's being invited (rather, told) to seek employment elsewhere. Each church has its own unique personality, as does each pastor. At times, bad

marriages take place between pastors and congregations. Each has high and often unrealistic expectations. The church expects the new pastor to be the answer to all its problems and the fulfiller of its dreams. With powerful preaching, dazzling personality, tireless visiting, flawless management, and shrewd planning, all the carefully watched statistical areas will soar. The pastor expects the people to follow his/her lead, to allow the pastor maximum freedom by making limited demands, to create no major problems, and to provide the financial base for the pastor's "program." At the least, the pastor expects cooperation, respect, enthusiastic acceptance, and some measure of control. Then, both begin to see the blemishes behind the other's make-up. The church folk may begin to think and say that the pastor really has not lived up to their early perception; the pastor is not "right" for them (or as one critic phrased it to his pastor, not "God's man" for the church); the pastor does not fit their situation. Out of a real and serious personality clash, the pastor can be forced to resign.

Sometimes all that is necessary for pastors to find themselves in deep trouble and with mounting pressure to move is to clash with powerful individuals in the church. This person can be male or female; rich, comfortable, or of modest means; deacon or organizational leader; or behind-the-scenes mover and shaker. Usually, this individual has been in the church for an extended time, is extremely active, has made a large circle of friends, and has carved out a niche of respectability and influence. Any of the following can trigger this person's hostile response: (1) The pastor's disagreeing with this individual. (2) The pastor's standing his/her ground on an issue instead of acquiescing to the individual. (3) The pastor's refusing the individual's request the pastor sincerely feels is not in the church's best interests. (4) The pastor's indicating the person will not receive preferential treatment. (5) The pastor's retaining the freedom to reject the individual's advice. (6) The pastor's failing to give the person a double portion of favor. To rile a powerful church member can create havoc in the pastoral world in the glaring of an eye. Make no mistake: To cross the wrong person, no matter how right the pastor may be, will start the wheels of pastoral dismissal rolling right over the unfortunate victim.

2. I believe most bad marriages between pastors and churches occur because one or both did not do enough, or good enough, homework during courtship. A failure to investigate can lead to crisis situations that end with pastors' being terminated. Prospective pastors owe it to themselves and their families to investigate the churches with which they are negotiating at least as thoroughly as the churches are investigating them. What are the churches' histories in the area of pastoral relations? Why did the former pastors leave? How have the churches provided for the needs of the pastors and their families? What are some of the problem areas in the churches? What are the congregations' expectations of their new pastors? What are some of the dreams and aspirations church members have for the churches? What is the churches' general attitudes toward outreach, ministry, and missions? Many pastors have come to grief because after they started their work in a new church, they began to discover factors they could have discovered in the negotiating stage.

The time to "negotiate the contract" is in discussions before the church calls the pastor. Salary, housing, off-days and vacation, general philosophy of ministry, study opportunities, indications of where the church wants to go—the pastor and the church need to understand each other on the front end. Investigation and negotiation will mean that the church will have a good idea of what to expect from the pastor, and the pastor will have realistic expectations of the church. The fewer the surprises down the road in pastor/church relations, the better.

Churches that do not check closely enough on pastors' relational, pulpit, caring, and administration skills may begin to feel cheated when the pastors do not "deliver" in one or more of these areas. Complaints accumulate, and pressure begins to build. The time for a pastoral change has come sooner rather than later.

An additional note is in order, I think. Search committees and prospective pastors need to be open and honest with each other. Also, no secret agreements should be made between a pastor search committee and a prospective pastor in contract negotiations. The contract is between the pastor and the congregation. For a church to discover somewhere down the line that certain unpublished agreements had been made with a search committee provides a basis for anger and mistrust. A credibility problem raises its ugly head and can result in the pastor's losing support—and ultimately the pastorate.

I believe at least one factor in pastoral terminations lies outside churches and pastors. Denominational programs can contribute to pastors' terminations. Inadvertently and unintentionally, I think, my denomination has contributed an element to the process that can result in pastoral terminations. That factor is the growth movement. Ironically, a valid emphasis on church growth (and I am all for growth) has placed tremendous pressure on some pastors who are not in situations that lend themselves to rapid growth. I am convinced that not all churches can experience significant, measurable growth—growth in terms of numbers on the church rolls. Again, one of my friends who was asked to resign his church was told his lack of dynamic leadership was responsible for his church's lack of growth. Totally ignored was the church's being located in a declining community. Some churches are in areas with shrinking populations and waning employment opportunities as industries cut back, shut down, or move out. Some pastors and churches must run as hard as they can merely to stay even.

In some churches with little growth, no growth, or decreasing numbers, members point to stories of swift, dramatic growth, ask the reason their church is not growing, and conclude their pastor is a fault. Many embattled pastors are doing all they know to do and are getting all the help they can, but without measurable success. In an effort at dialoging and brainstorming, they ask their people, "How can our church grow?" Sometimes the response is, "How should we know? That's your job. Do it." If current pastors cannot lead in or produce growth, churches can and do replace them.

Conveniently and tragically, other factors in a pastor's ministry are ignored because they are difficult to tote up on a scoreboard. Many pastors in non-growth situations have given deeply of themselves in a caring ministry that has helped people through their valleys of deep shadow. These servant-pastors have contributed to the spiritual growth of Christians who have learned that the high calling to service comes to every believer. Members of congregations have grown from spiritual infants into effective leaders under the wise and patient nurture of a caring pastor. How do you put numbers on such significant contributions?

Other elements likely are involved in the dynamics that lead to pastors' being terminated. My list is not exhaustive, but I think it represents major factors in the crisis that continues unabated among Southern Baptists. A reading of the causes I have mentioned will suggest readily that in many cases more than one element comes into play. The situation is complex; the pastoral field is sown with numerous land mines waiting to be touched off. I feel that if pastors are aware of at least some of the mines, they can anticipate problems that never occurred to me and can move to deal with them before they create the explosive crisis of termination. Pastors can work on the factors or elements before they begin to work against him.

Churches can become aware of their tendencies and expectations; they can put names on some of the currents of our culture that too easily are brought over into the body of Christ and adopted without close examination. These elements of culture can replace the search for Christ's will and can drown out the still, small voice trying to be heard. Together, pastors and churches can work for the good of Christ's cause, in which both are servants.

Chapter 5

Deadly Deficiencies

A Defective Approach

Nothing in my background or training prepared me adequately for the severe crisis I endured in my pastoral ministry. I must shoulder a large share of the blame for this because of my inadequate view of my role as pastor. A second contributing factor was a lack of guidance in crucial aspects of ministering in a local congregation.

As I reflect, I flinch at how naive I was as I prepared to move into the challenging work of leading a church. I deeply wanted to be the best pastor possible. As I worked toward a doctorate in the field of New Testament, I kept my options open. If an opportunity came to teach on the college or eventually on the seminary level, I wanted to be ready. If the Lord led me into the pastoral ministry, where I felt the strongest pull, I would be content to work there as long as I could. My views of a pastor's role and people's responses to it, however, were woefully naive and inadequate.

I remember reaching the conclusion early on that if I studied hard at sermon preparation, honed what teaching skills I had, worked at ministering to needs, and consistently visited members and prospective members, I would develop as a pastor and satisfy most people's expectations. I had no illusions about being a superlative or even near-riveting pulpiteer. I felt I was at least adequate as a teacher. I was confident I could develop skills in counseling, hospital and nursing-home ministry, and relational skills in working with members of a congregation. If I worked diligently in those areas, what could go wrong that would threaten me severely? The thought of being opposed personally rarely surfaced as a prominent concern.

Second, I assumed that as a pastor called to a church, I would have leadership—some degree of authority and power—by virtue of that call and my role. Only later would I learn I would have to earn leadership. When, and if, church folk decided to let me lead, I would be given some measure of authority. Moreover, I discovered that the church of which I was pastor might decide not to bestow the mantle of leadership on me.

Third, I did not take into account that not all the saints would be kindly disposed, tolerant, forgiving, and patient with me—or with one another, for that matter. Mercifully, many members of congregations are supportive and caring. Their prayers and participation enable their pastors to do their often difficult work. Yet for pastors to assume that most members of their congregations will give them the benefit of the doubt— "cut them some slack" —is for pastors to set themselves up for trouble.

Finally, I had a fairly strong sense of being protected by the One who had called me to serve Him. I never expected Him to shield me from all problems and difficulties; I did not think He would make me immune or invulnerable to all bumps and bruises. I did believe that whatever came, He and I could handle it. As long as I was in His will, things would work out. I did not expect the ministerial road to be smooth and easy, but I did not expect to find myself in the valley of the shadow of pastoral death, either. I still am embarrassed when I face the shallowness of my thinking and the incredible slowness with which I picked up on danger signals and ways of responding to them.

Insufficient Preparation

My formal training really did not prepare me in some crucial areas of the pastoral ministry. In all probability, courses were offered in seminary that I did not take because I felt they had little to do with my goals. I took a course in pastoral ministries that dealt with various areas of a pastor's work. The course in psychology that was required in my core curriculum was called "Personality Development." Yet these and other course offerings either did not provide crucial insights and warnings or I missed needed input altogether. I may have failed to note other areas of study that would have equipped me better to understand, relate to, and deal with the wide variety of people in any given congregation. I remember no pointers on how to spot and to deal with power structures and dangerous individuals who were explosives with short fuses waiting for a flame.

I still have a seminary bulletin from the period when I was in graduate school. Courses offered that applied to dealing with people were one on understanding adults, one on personality development, and one on interpersonal relationships in the church. Only a course in personality development was listed in the required courses for the basic theological degree. Perhaps if I had inquired, I could have been steered in directions that would have prepared me better, yet looking back, I was woefully unequipped in the area of the dynamics at work in any given congregation.

I became interested in what is being done now to equip pastors-to-be to understand themselves better and to relate to people in their churches. A survey of seminary catalogues revealed courses on individual analysis, stress management (could I have ever used that one!), survival skills for ministers (ditto!), career support for ministers, Christian leadership and change management, career assessment, and ministry development. Obviously, something is being done to help potential pastors. My guess is that as pastoral firings continue to escalate, even more attention will be given to pastors' relating to their congregations.

The advice I received that has remained with me through the years was good but totally inadequate. In one of my courses, the professor said, in essence: "Remember, don't put your hands on the women church members, don't misuse the church's money, and don't mismanage your own money." To commit these acts would be to commit serious wrongs that would warrant criticism and dismissal. I assumed that if I avoided even the appearance of these evils, I would eliminate the prime causes of losing a pastorate. No one told me that good pastors have lost their vocational lives for a lot less than any of the three ministerial no-no's. Not much is required to trigger "righteous indignation" in any number of people in the average congregation. With one light push of the right button, the dismissal machinery is set in motion.

Early in my ministry, I served in a pastoral internship. If I had enjoyed a close, personal relationship with an experienced pastor—a kind of Paul-Timothy, student-mentor relationship—I would have been helped greatly to understand and to cope with various types of church folk. For a number of reasons beyond my control, I did not have that crucial advantage. I worked under the leading of two pastors, one of whom was dealing with his crisis situation. When he retired suddenly and another pastor came, I was a left-over staff member who did not quite fit in with the new regime. After a while, I was "encouraged" to take one of two opportunities I had open to me to become a pastor (whether or not I felt God's leading to do so). Thus, in retrospect, my formal schooling and my pastoral internship left me with critical voids, a number of blank spaces, that later would contribute to my long night without song.

A Lack of Awareness

During my struggle for pastoral survival, I was helped to recognize church personality types with explosive potential, thanks in large part to George Cox, the hospital chaplain I introduced earlier. My heightened awareness came too late, but it helped me understand how I was blind-sided so easily and the dominant traits of some of the people out to get me. I realized that from the beginning of my ministerial journey, I had encountered representatives of the various potentially dangerous personality types. New and deeper understanding would stand me in good stead, whether I continued in the pastorate or moved to some other vocation.

Some saints-in-good-standing constantly stoke the fires of **anger** within. They are angry most of the time, although they probably are unaware of their dominant emotion or mood. Anger is their favorite feeling. They feel best when they are mad at somebody or about something. Much of the time, they likely will not be able to pinpoint the reason they are angry or at precisely what or whom their anger is directed. They have collected a mass of free-floating anger. They have a whole load of anger ready to dump on an available victim. They well may be angry with marriage partners because the spouses have not fulfilled certain imposed expectations or with children because they will not fit into the molds set up for them. Their anger may be directed at coworkers because they do not recognize the angry people's abilities or follow their directives and advice. They may be angry with employers because they do not give well-deserved promotions and recognitions or with friends because they do not give proper attention or support. All these people may serve as convenient targets for a deep-rooted and carefully nurtured anger fed by a realization they are not who and where they aspired to be in life.

Things are not going right or feeling right with people nurturing anger and someone else is to blame. They might be angry with God because they feel He has done something to them, has allowed something negative to happen to them, or has not given a requested blessing. Because they do not dare lash out at God, they can do the next best thing: They can get at God's representative, the pastor. So at the first, slightest pretext—and a pastor's work makes a ready supply of pretexts available—the angry saints unleash their anger. They have found an open, vulnerable target. They may feel good most of the time now, for they can feel angry about an almost endless number of things their pastor does or does not do.

Some church members are **jealously protective** of their status within the congregation. Many Christians serve with the clear, worthy motive of pleasing and honoring Christ. Others, however, have and constantly nurture a deep sense of having "arrived" at a cherished goal. Interestingly, they are hard workers. They have put a great deal of time and effort into getting to a certain level in the church. They are deacons, members of important committees, and directors of major church organizations. Their roles mean a great deal to them because their church status makes up for a lack (or lacks) in their lives. They may not have a high-ranking, well paying, or highly visible job; the most beautiful house; this year's model of a leading car; the best education; or the finest clothes. They have, however, made their places in their churches.

The "church achievers" enjoy the attention they receive; the surging sense of authority, acclaim, and importance their position gives; the feeling that, in their church, they have their peers' approval, acceptance, and respect. Their self-images may take a beating in other arenas, but in their churches they are "somebodies."

Make no mistake, church members whose identities hinge largely on their status in their congregations are extremely protective of their niches. Any perceived threat to the places they have carved out for themselves meets with immediate and strong reaction. Anything the pastor says or does that they interpret as a step to replace them in their cherished roles will be met with some form of counter offensive. Perhaps the pastor does not give them perceived due recognition for their contributions, or does not call on them to lead some of the church's major projects, or does not suggest them for notable roles in worship or other church activities. Or, they simply may feel the pastor is not friendly enough to them, which they see as a slight, a put-down, or a sign their grips on their niches are slipping. They cannot and will not let anybody take away what they have worked so long and hard to acquire and secure.

In any congregation, I am convinced, are members with a deep need to **control.** This coin has two sides. Some people do not feel in charge anywhere else, but they have found in a congregational-type of church government a place to work at having a strong voice in what takes place. They cannot control the economic situation in which they feel caught; others have the power in the areas of employment, job assignments, salaries, and promotions. People with a need to control have little or no voice in setting tax rates or in legislating laws. Some are not in control in their families. They cannot change their spouses—fashion them into their own concepts of ideal (and manageable) marriage partners. Their spouses insist on retaining their own personalities and some measures of individuality. The children of people seeking control will not shape up to their parents' standards and ideas either.

Frustrated church members bent on exercising control in *something* often cannot seem to get their lives together and are thwarted in trying to have a hand in directing others' lives. In their churches, however, they can let their strong opinions and feelings be known about any decision the congregation is considering. They can find others who feel as they do, and they subtly can manipulate matters at times. This gives the control-seekers satisfaction when they "win" and leaves them disgruntled when they "lose." They desperately want to be in charge somewhere, and they have chosen the church as their best, and maybe only, chance. If these individuals come to view their pastors as barriers to at least a measure of control, they have to do something about the pastors, whom they may view as rivals for control or as actually having the highly coveted control.

The other side of the coin is that some church members do exercise measures of control at home and at work. These people assume they can be in control in their churches and so they assert themselves.

Some individuals in every congregation **demand** to be seen, heard, and served. They delight in making their demands and having those demands met. They are needy and dependent. Most often, these people identify themselves soon after a new pastor arrives at their church. They make it their business to buttonhole their pastors at the first opportunity. Their pastors need to know who they are, and they need to know whether the pastors will play their game. A demanding church member may begin with soft subtly: A cousin twice removed is in a local hospital. When the pastor makes his rounds, would he drop in and visit the cousin? Of course, the pastor is not asked to go out of his way, but the member would appreciate his making the visit. Actually, the demanding member is making more than a request; it is a directive and a test. The church member will be sure to ask the cousin whether the pastor stopped by to visit. Whether the cousin is a member of another local church that is ministering to the person, and no matter how distant or out of the way the hospital might be, demanding church member's primary concern is that the pastor please him or her. If the pastor does not comply with the "request," demanding member's next approach is more direct, something to the effect of "You haven't been by to see my relative." The words are an accusation; the implication is that the pastor is negligent.

I became involved in a classic case of the demand-and-respond game in my assistant pastor's role on a church staff. A long-time, vocal, chip-on-his-shoulder church member met me coming down one of the halls in the church's educational space. In essence, and without prelude, he said: "You and the pastor have not been by the hospital to visit my mother" (who was a member of another church in the city). He made no request; he asked no questions; he made no allowances. He made a direct charge of dereliction of duty. I responded that I knew nothing about his mother's being hospitalized. He countered that he had called the church office and had given the receptionist the information. The not-so-subtle demand was that the pastor and I had better get on the job and be in his mother's hospital room on the double. We complied, and the church member had the satisfaction of another fulfilled demand.

A demanding saint may take another approach: "Pastor, I don't mind if you don't visit my family, because I know you're busy. But go by to visit widow Jones every chance you get. Because of her age and health, she can't get out much; but she needs our church's ministry." Underneath is the message: "You had better visit us *and* widow Jones." Not to do either is to fail the test and lose the game.

Demanding church members get a kind of pay-off when others do as they demand, when others jump through the designated hoops in responding to the stated directives. Demanding members of congregations really like to give orders. They do not have any other platforms for giving directions; but as members of their churches they feel they have every right to expect their pastors to do as they say. If pastors move quickly to satisfy the demands, the game is underway and will continue; and those who delight in it will go on receiving their pay-offs.

Some members of congregations live with a lingering feeling of **frustration.** God, life, and people have let them down. They have reached a point in life where they must face an awful truth: They are not where they planned to be this juncture in their lives, and chances do not look good that they will reach their goals. This is probably as far as they will go; they will have to adjust to lower levels of achievement and finances. Reshaping their dreams is painful. In their frustration, they well may resent the pastor's status and level of attainment, especially if they think the pastor's salary level exceeds theirs. The pastor becomes a handy target for their frustrations.

Individuals in churches often accumulate and carry a sense of a high degree of **power.** Their rise to leadership positions may have occurred because of their wealth, professional positions, length of service in the church, and number of friends. However, they attained power, others in the congregation take their cue from the powerful people, who become power brokers in the church. Others watch for these brokers' signals of how they want church matters decided. People with power become accustomed to other members' currying their favor. For pastors not to recognize who wields the power and fall in line is to court disaster.

Other walking land mines populate most congregations. Some members vie to be their pastors' favorites; they constantly want the pastors' time and attention; they hang on every assurance that they have the pastors' attention and response. When these members sense they are not receiving the favoritism they seek, they quickly turn on pastors whom they view as refusing to give them what they want. Many of them had not been their fathers' favorite children; for pastors to give signals these church members are not his favorites ignites long-held resentment and anger.

Other church members play a deadly game of "guess what I need." These saints do not inform their pastors of individual and family needs. When pastors do not anticipate or guess those needs and meet them, the disgruntled members lower the boom. Also sprinkled among congregations are "theologians" who feel constrained to test their pastors' views and biblical interpretations. They may be self-taught or formerly trained, and they stay poised to challenge sermons and teachings that go counter to their positions. Some church members like to nurture hurt feelings. Their pastors or other members have not treated them right. They carefully stoke their hurt feelings with a list of real or imagined slights and offenses. Pastors who do not recognize and soothe such hurts frequently become seen as the prime offenders.

All the types of people I have described in congregations are persons with needs to whom sensitive, caring pastors will seek to minister. They also pose delicate problems pastors will do well to identify and of which they must remain aware.

My purpose has been to lay out part of the mine field through which pastors must make their way. I would be remiss, however, if I did not stress the delightful, helpful, and caring types of people who also make up congregations. Some are encouragers who will love and be loyal to their pastors because of their high view of the pastoral role. Some are faithful in attendance and monetary giving with no thought of recognition. Others are generous in giving of themselves—their time, energies, and skills—out of compassion for others and concern for the effectiveness of their churches' ministries. Members with the gift of relating visit consistently on their churches' behalf, inviting people to church functions and seeking to establish relationships with new friends. Christians with a wide variety of professional skills use those skills in areas of law, finance, and medical (especially emergency) assistance to help their churches. Those with practical know-how help meet maintenance needs and take part in volunteer missions projects that involve building houses and places of worship. These are only some of the folk who offer hope and inspiration to a pastor and who move the church toward realizing its mission and purpose.

I did not do well in my attempt to tiptoe through the mine fields. A large part of the fault was mine. Some of the people-types easily and quickly hooked me into playing their games. I remember warmly and with gratitude the others who enriched my life.

Lack of Peer Support

Whether real or imagined, I felt that outside the support group and some friends, I received little peer support. Perhaps some of the other pastors who knew me did not know about my crisis or, if they knew, did not know its severity. Maybe some knew and did not want to become involved or were too busy. I have the feeling some were threatened by what was happening to me. They could be next.

I had rather think that most of my fellow pastors really did not know what to do or say. If so, somehow pastors need some insights on how to minister to one another, especially those in trouble: written or verbal encouragement; use of contacts to help embattled pastors move; prayer support; physical presence whenever possible in order to listen; and alerting hurting pastors to sources of help on the associational, state, and denominational level. Shunning the potentially pastoral unemployed deepens the threatened pastors' anguish; help offers hope and assists troubled pastors to retain a positive view of the pastoral role. Fellow pastors have marvelous opportunities to minister to their hurting brothers; they can be pastors to pastors.

Placement System

One of the factors that militates against a Southern Baptist pastor facing termination is the method of identifying potential pastors and eventually calling them in a congregational type of church government. First, churches are reluctant to consider seriously a pastor who is in trouble or who has been terminated. Most churches want pastors who are happy where they are, have all the wheels on the wagon well-oiled and turning, and must be persuaded that the new challenge merits a ministerial move. Of course, this is understandable. Fired or about-to-be-terminated pastors, however, certainly are not viewed as successful. Thus, they make poor candidates for churches seeking new pastors. My hunch is that most of the time the cause of a recommended pastor's trouble or of his termination is secondary or remains unexamined. That the pastor was fired because of the whims of a congregation or a disgruntled element in the church makes little if any difference. Firing, whether legitimate or not, carries a damaging and sometimes fatal stigma the pastor must bear.

Pressured pastors have the cards stacked against them. They cannot apply for a job with a church. They might send their resumes to churches, but search committees well may view their doing so as self-promotion and quickly disregard them. Even if aspirants respond to churches' want-ads in Baptist state papers, their terminations are huge strikes against them. Terminated Baptist pastors have no director of a placement system who can move them quickly. The pastor must be recommended to a search committee who, in turn, may investigate, listen to a sermon, and conduct an interview. The committee may or may not pursue the matter. If not, the process begins again. Sometimes, months stretch into years. In the case of a terminated pastor-friend mentioned earlier, four years went by before he received an opportunity to resume full-time pastoral ministry.

Baptists' lack of some means of placing their pastors in a reasonable time creates a vast number of victims and contributes to the continuing exodus of men from the pastoral ministry or to the sanctuary of other denominations. Some do not want to leave their denomination; but for them and their families to survive, they must go elsewhere to minister and earn a livelihood. I do not have the answer to the problem. I do not have in mind an ideal placement system that retains God's role in calling and moving pastors and at the same time helps troubled pastors and churches. Yet we must give much more attention to some means of retaining people who feel strongly their call is to be pastors but who face or have experienced termination.

Emerging Corrections

Happily, some of the deficiencies in dealing with the problem of pastoral terminations are being corrected. Earlier, I alluded to seminary courses that help prepare a pastor for stress and conflict. Some denominations offer seminars in personal and professional growth and have turned attention to the epidemic of pastoral terminations. Denominational and state publications have helped raise the consciousness of more people concerning the plight of a growing number of pastors. Respected denominational leaders continue to call attention to the rising tide of pastoral firings. Some state conventions have set up emergency funds to help pastors who have been terminated.

We must do everything possible to promote kindness, patience, compassion, and grace on the part of pressured pastors and troubled churches in and following conflict; we must look for redemptive ways to make needed changes in churches' pastoral leadership. The key word is *redemptive*—a positive course of action for pastors and churches. One such available redemptive resource is mediation and intentional interims. We need to continue to work at correcting deadly deficiencies in institutions, potential pastors, and churches if we are to reverse the trend in pastoral terminations and thereby salvage persons and ministries.

Chapter 6

Elements of Hope

Suggested Actions Pastors Can Take

Most pastors must make their way through a complex maze of pressures, demands, and multiple responsibilities. All except the favored few who are so successful and popular they can write their own contracts are pulled and pushed from every direction as they try to steer a steady course in their many-faceted ministries. What are some of the actions pastors can take to anticipate and prevent causes of and excuses for termination? The following are representative suggestions; they are not intended to be exhaustive.

1. In private conversations, sermons, devotionals, and public prayers, pastors can indicate their realization that they are unfinished products on whom God still is at work, shaping and molding them. They can indicate they constantly are working at developing their own styles and philosophies of ministry; they are seeking to move toward spiritual maturity. They can ask members of their congregations to give them objective and constructive feedback concerning ways they can minister more effectively to church members. Pastors can express an openness to suggestions about better ways they can meet members' needs.

Under the heading "Lessons Too-Late Learned" were two that came after I made the transition from pulpit to pew. On two occasions, in their first addresses to us as their congregation two newly called pastors did what I wished I had done as a new pastor. The first told us what we could expect of him, one element of which was consistent sermon preparation. In essence, he said he made no claim to be among the elite as a preacher, but his promise to us was that he never would enter the pulpit to preach without being prepared. He consistently delivered on his promise, steadily enhancing his credibility. (Plus, he was an excellent preacher.) The second new pastor, in the course of beginning his ministry among us, stated that he would make mistakes but asked that we be patient and deal openly with him about them so we could move on together as pastor and people. His honesty and confession of humanness contributed to his getting off to a good start. To be up front concerning what churches can expect and confessing to be less than perfect while being open to dialogue would have stood me in good stead. Doing so will begin to establish a bond between pastors and churches that pastors can continue to strengthen.

2. Pastors can determine that if charges should be leveled against them, one will not be their failure to work hard and consistently at being good ministers. They will hustle, first because of their sense of divine call, then because of personal integrity. If/when they make mistakes, those mistakes will occur in the course of diligent effort; they will not be the inexcusable mistakes of doing nothing (or as little as possible). Pastors will do their work to the best of their ability and consistently because they first are working for their Lord and because they genuinely care for people. A by-product of their efforts will be a strong defense against the charge of shirking their duties as pastors.

3. By their honesty, openness, sense of fairness, strong work-ethic, and readiness to relate, pastors can gain or reestablish respect for their role. They can remove the "freeloader" image some church members have of pastors.

4. Pastors can become knowledgeable of their churches' histories and present concepts of themselves, views of the churches' ministries, and dreams of the churches' futures. Such knowledge will allow pastors to relate to their churches' unique personalities. At the same time, pastors can work patiently and tactfully toward needed changes. They can be aware that, generally, people resist change. Thus, changes in churches' directions and ministries usually come slowly as people follow the lead of pastors who have established credibility. As I learned the hard way, trying to implement change too quickly is to invite trouble. As in so much else in life, in effecting needed change in churches "timing is everything."

Personality clashes with church members are inevitable. When such clashes occur, they need immediate attention. Pastors may need to alert proper leadership (staff, personnel committee, deacons), to begin discussions with the persons involved, and to indicate a willingness to relate while refusing to compromise convictions of conscience. Pastors' openness to dialogue is key.

5. Pastors can work with their staff members and/or church councils to provide visitation opportunities for church members. Pastors can adopt an outreach stance in sermons and writings that will indicate they are open to avenues of church growth and that all church members have roles in church growth.

Along with an outreach emphasis, pastors can lead in and promote inreach—reclaiming inactive church members and ministering to their congregations' genuine needs. A healthy balance needs to be maintained between outreach and spiritual nurture, between an emphasis on growth in numbers and growth toward spiritual maturity. Pastors can stress the "both-and" nature of their churches' task.

6. As has been touched on earlier, prospective pastors can give themselves an essential break by learning all they can about churches that are considering calling them. At the same time churches are "looking over" prospective pastors, the "candidates" should be looking closely at the churches. Prospective pastors can be "up-front" with search committees in stating they are learning all they can about the church. If this causes the committees to become nervous, the signal may be that the churches have something to hide and that the "candidates" for pastor well may be on the verge of swapping one problem-laden situation for another. If, however, the search committees' responses are positive and open, negotiations can move to a new and refreshing level. Pastors owe it to themselves, their families, and their ministries to examine closely churches that are interested in talking with them about a move.

Prospective pastors are well served to write their questions and ask them of search committees. They also can talk to state leaders and former pastors of the churches. Prospective pastors can visit interested churches' worship periods unannounced, as part of the congregations, to get a feel for the churches. Prospective pastors can ask to review the churches' previous year's records to get an idea of the church's strengths and weaknesses. Such research will not forestall all problems, but it certainly will cut down considerably on negative surprises.

7. When conflicts arise between pastors and staff members, pastors first can seek to talk out differences in an effort to reach an understanding. One-on-one discussion—open frankness and real listening—will establish and keep open avenues of communication and will demonstrate sincerity of effort to resolve difficulties. If resolution is not achieved, pastors can take the matter to the church leaders so that negotiations may proceed with a tone of openness instead of threat. Pastors need to make every effort not to assume an adversarial roll but a mediating, redemptive role. The tone of threat has to be avoided. All along, the willingness of pastors to be flexible and fair must be evident; and the work of the churches must be put before personal preferences. Priority must be placed on doing what is redemptive for the churches, the staff members, and the pastors.

The dismissal of staff members merely on the basis of the pastors' preferences does not lie within the scope of this brief book, but it is an area I feel needs immediate and serious attention among Southern Baptists. To tell a church's staff members an incoming pastor wants to bring a preexisting staff or wants to build a new staff, or to allow pastors to fire staff members at will negates God's call of and will for those staff members. Many times, such firings are done without the larger congregations' knowledge or approval. Pushing resident staff members out into the night on short notice is not my idea of respecting their sense of calling and expresses decided lack of care.

8. Pastors may request that their churches' personnel committees act as liaison committees between the congregations and pastors. These groups can confer regularly with pastors about potential problem areas that begin to surface. An alternate approach would be establishing three- or four-member liaison committees to act as buffers and as channels of communication between pastors and congregations. These groups can handle minor problems and move to meet potentially major difficulties. These committees also can encourage open dialogue between

pastors and members who have questions or criticisms. If such a system runs smoothly, church members know they have a forum where they can be heard; and members prone to begin "campaigns" against pastors can be reminded they have a ready means to air their concerns or grievances. This approach does not suggest pastors' study doors are not open when members need to see them; it does offer pastors protection from relatively minor problems that consume their time and drain their energy—and that otherwise could grow into major difficulties.

9. Pastors can help themselves immeasurably by developing relationships of deep trust with a mature, sensitive church member who will reflect accurately the congregation's "state of mind." Admittedly, a risk is involved in doing this, for the trusted persons may betray confidences or even may turn on the pastors somewhere along the way. Thus, time and careful observation must precede the risk of personal trust. If the individuals have the interests of their churches and pastors at heart, those persons can alert the pastors to simmering difficulties before they boil over. This will allow pastors to take the initiative to deal with the problems instead of being blindsided. Pastors can be proactive instead of reactive.

10. Pastors can make every effort to keep themselves physically fit, emotionally healthy, and mentally alert. They will continue to have birthdays like everyone else; and they will not find the fountain of youth. Yet they can take steps to prevent becoming old before their time. Stagnation is unnecessary and unacceptable. The older pastors become, the more they must place accent on being active; their pace may slow somewhat, but their schedule must include hours outside the office among church members, no matter how many staff members their churches may have.

11. The longer pastors stay at their churches, the more they must focus on injecting freshness into what they do. They do well to vary their preaching, study and read as widely as possible, and be aware of new ministry ideas that have possibilities for their churches. They must look for creative ways to promote internal fellowship, maintain their personal devotional life, and be aggressive in seeking to relate to church members as individuals.

12. Even if pastors have liaison committees "with an ear to the ground" to identify potential problems (suggestion 8), they need to keep their antennae out for signs of unrest. This does not mean pastors become defensive, pessimistic, or negative. It does mean that rather than wait for the unpleasant surprises, they are sensitive to currents and cross currents in their congregations so they can be prepared to act decisively and yet kindly. They need to observe keenly and listen intently.

13. Pastors can find and relate to a mentor. I believe every pastor needs a pastor, even as every counselor needs a counselor. To find and establish a close relationship with an older, more experienced pastor—perhaps a retired pastor—within easy visiting distance will prove to be invaluable. To tap into the store of accumulated wisdom gained over years and through hard knocks allows a younger pastor to avoid dangerous pitfalls. Having a wise, accessible pastor-friend does not mean never being pushed to the wall. It does mean that chances for survival, endurance, and continuing productive ministry will be heightened.

14. Finally, pastors can cultivate at least one friend outside their churches and outside a religious vocation who will care, listen, observe, and then respond in objective, blunt honesty. Such a friend offers a relationship in which pastors can be themselves without anxiety about image. They can have the benefit of objective evaluation of circumstances, motives, methods, people, and possible courses of action. As I indicated earlier, my hospital-chaplain friend filled this role for me and suggested that all pastors need "outside" friends who will not let their pastor-friends mire themselves in self-deception, self-pity, or self-recrimination. In addition, outside friends can give needed insights about what makes church people "tick."

Pastors can, and must, help themselves and give themselves every possible advantage in spotting, sizing up, and moving to cope with potential difficulties and difficult people. Not to do so is to run the extremely dangerous risk of vulnerability that invites disaster.

Suggested Actions Churches Can Take

I have a deep, abiding love and respect for local churches. A small but strong church in a small southern Mississippi town nurtured and helped shape me during my formative years. People there invested part of their lives in me, and I am indebted to them. That congregation and ensuing local churches helped equip me for ministry and gave me opportunities to minister as a staff member and as a pastor. Now, as a layperson, I worship and serve in a local church in which my wife and I are included in an incredible depth of fellowship and are enriched by warm relationships.

I am grateful that for about 14 years, I had opportunities to serve on church staffs and to fill a pastoral role. Then, as an employee of LifeWay Christian Resources of the Southern Baptist Convention, for more than 20 years I was privileged to edit Bible study materials for local churches. Since retirement, I have enjoyed opportunities to write those materials. All along that journey, a great part of the motivation and purpose of my work has been to serve Christ and to help local churches reach people for Christ and then nurture them in the faith. High on the list of my heroes are laypersons who give liberally of themselves in their churches, motivated by a love for Christ and people and by a deep desire to serve their Lord.

I am convinced beyond argument that hope for our world, for the society in which we live, and for my denomination lies in local churches' vital ministries. If lives are transformed and nurtured toward spiritual maturity and effective service, local churches will get the job done. Christ still is working through colonies of committed Christians in a society steadily becoming more pagan. In every local church, one can find dedicated, loving, caring believers who want most of all to serve Christ by serving people—all people in need of His saving and sustaining grace.

The flip side of the coin is that many churches need a renewed vision of mission, a new vitality, and a new determination to change our culture rather than being changed by it. A number of elements, I think, will be necessary for renewal: prayer for God's forgiveness, strength, and guidance; a determined search for and commitment to His will and purpose; a new respect and love for others in the Christian community—a renewed concept of believers as a family of faith; a deeper sense of the seriousness of people's being separated from God; a new sense of responsibility to "always be prepared to give an answer to everyone who asks [us] to give the reason for the hope that [we] have" (1 Pet. 3:15); and a strong drive to minister to broken and hurting people.

I firmly believe that part of any effective renewal for local churches will be their reevaluations of church-pastor relations. One of the things churches will have to do, in my opinion, is to examine their view of the pastoral role and to weigh their willingness to enhance that role, no matter who is filling it at a particular time. Churches need to provide as best they can for their pastors' needs, and churches must demand and draw from their pastors the best that is in them. What churches expect from their pastors must be matched by support for pastors. A new and stronger partnership must be formed in which churches and pastors feel themselves called to serve together in a complementary relationship. Pastors will lead in equipping the saints for the work of ministry (Eph. 4:11-12). In turn, members of congregations will support, encourage, pray for, and work with their pastors.

What are actions churches consciously and deliberately can take to develop and maintain healthy, productive relationships with their pastors? Representative suggestions are:

1. Churches with histories of outright firing or pressuring pastors to resign well may need to spend time and effort to determine the mind-set behind that tendency. (The flip side of that coin is that pastors who repeatedly find themselves "in hot water" with their churches need to take close looks at themselves to determine their tendencies.) Granted, unfortunate incidents occur in which churches have legitimate reasons to call for pastors' resignations. If situations of pressured resignations and forced terminations become repeated incidents in a church's life, however, some of the blame must be shifted from pastors to the church. What in a church's make-up or attitude toward pastors gives rise to a proneness to dismiss pastors? One major factor in any church's health is the willingness and ability to deal redemptively with

problems involving pastoral leadership. The word, both good and bad, spreads: A church "chews up and spits out" pastors, or the church handles difficulties involving pastors maturely out of concern for the church's and the pastor's ministries.

Somewhere in my night without song, I was preparing to leave a church member's home after a pastoral visit. She and her sister were caring for their aging, ailing mother. The lady was one of the most courageous people of faith I have known. As she saw me out, she indicated she was aware of my trouble. Then she said, in essence: "You're not the first pastor they have mistreated." Tragically, I later was a member of a church that also developed a history of treating pastors roughly.

As in the case with pastors, a priority of all churches should be to honor the Lord of the church. For churches, image may not be everything, but their reputations need to convey something of the love, compassion, and kindness of their Lord. People notice.

2. Church members can devote time and energy to working toward a clear understanding of what they want to be and to do as local expressions of the body of Christ. Do members see themselves as a servant church? as open to receive all people who come to worship and have a desire to join the fellowship? as a family of God with strong ties of grace and love? What opportunities of ministry are open where the church facilities are located and from which members scatter to serve? Are members really interested in reaching out to people around them? What place does missions involvement hold in the church's list of priorities?

Churches need a clear concept of their identity and mission. Through the deacon body, the church council, the Sunday School council, and open-forum discussions, churches can hammer out clear expressions of their self-understanding, goals, and dreams.

The vital exercise of a church's determining its identity and mission will help a pastor on the scene or one who comes later to lead in facilitating methods and approaches that move toward realization of the church's goals. The pastor does not have to "sell" a program; church members do not have to be persuaded to "buy into" someone else's plan because they can feel ownership from the start. Likely, the more people who have opportunity for input, the more who will take part in the church's work.

At the front end, a pastor will have crucial insight into how a church feels about itself, the direction it is going, and the goals toward which it is moving. Particularly in the negotiating stage between a church and a prospective pastor, the pastor under consideration will have valuable information that will help in determining whether the person's personality, skills, and approach to ministry fit a particular church. Such crucial information also will enable a prospective pastor to note areas in which positive change needs to take place with time, patience, tact, love, and persuasive leadership from a base of credibility and proven integrity.

3. Churches can arrive at and state expectations of their pastors. What do they see as their pastors' major tasks? What is their first priority in the skills they want their pastors to have? What specific, immediate needs do they want their pastors to address? What kind of office schedule do they expect their pastors to have?

The most well prepared pastor search committees I talked with knew what their churches wanted in a pastor—what they wanted the individual to do immediately and then long-range. Some committees, however, had surprising priorities. One congregation had built a beautiful new sanctuary, and their priority concern was calling a pastor who could motivate members' giving so they could get out from under a sizeable debt. Another church's priority requirement was a pastor who would visit members on a regular basis. A third church wanted someone who was skilled in counseling; members viewed this as major need and as the church's foremost ministry. Still another church was looking for a pastor who would "stay on the field" the majority of the time; they wanted the pastor to be available to members. Looking back, these were legitimate as elements in a list of priorities but at least in some cases probably were not the top priorities for churches to have. Yet at least the committees were clear in what their churches were seeking.

The least-prepared pastor-search committee with whom I met seemed to have no clue about how to conduct a conversation or ask questions about me, my family, or my approach to ministry. At lunch, after a lengthy lull, I had to take the lead in conducting the meeting. The committee's lack of adequate preparation taught me that churches must spend time equipping their search committees. Merely because sincere, dedicated people have been Christians and church members for many years does not mean they are equipped to be on search committees. With training, however, these folk can offer excellent service in a church's process of selecting a pastor.

"As clearly as we can determine, here is what our people want from their pastor:" Such open expressions of expectations are invaluable and crucial in a prospective pastor's being able to compare skills and approach to ministry with a church's wants and needs. Such openness can help prevent bad marriages of pastors and churches—and the tragic aftermath of contentious divorces.

4. Churches can gain and continue to retain a real sense that pastors are called to minister where they feel God has placed them. Churches who seek God's will in calling pastors need to respect the selected pastors' conviction that God has led them to accept the churches' invitations. Likely, the first priority of most pastors—of all serious, committed pastors—is to be where God wants them to be. They diligently look for and seek to follow God's leading. Churches can seek the pastors God has for them and feel that God has a hand in the selection process. This will prevent a "hired-hand" approach to the pastor's role and will stress the element of God's leading both the church and the pastor in an effective partnership in ministry.

Retaining the element of God's calling in pastor-church relations makes possible redemptive approaches to differences and difficulties. Such retention will mean that problems in the relationship will be handled with prayer and a desire for what is best for both and for the advancement of God's work. Dialogue and negotiation will replace complaints and angry ultimatums. Respect for the pastoral role can be maintained no matter who is filling the role at a given time in the church's history, and no matter what the problems that must be dealt with as redemptively as possible.

5. Churches can (and should) provide adequately for their pastors' financial needs. Doing so is scriptural. When Jesus sent his

disciples on mission for Him, He told them that "the worker deserves his wages" (Luke 10:7). Although Paul worked to support himself to counter any charge that he preached for money, he championed the right of others to receive monetary support: "The Lord has commanded that those who preach the gospel should receive their living from the gospel" (1 Cor. 9:14).

To my mind, pastors should not expect to live on a level above their congregations; but neither should they be expected to live on a level below members of their churches, as though living by faith means pastors can get by on less. A pastor's financial needs parallel other people's needs: food, clothing, transportation, housing, insurance, books, children's college funds, and retirement provisions. Pastors receive no divine dispensation of dollars; their heavenly treasure is not converted into earthly currency.

Most churches expect their pastors to dress well, maintain a presentable and functioning automobile, purchase resources for continuing study, live in attractive houses that are furnished tastefully, and pay their bills on time. All this takes as much money for pastors as for anyone else.

One of the most stunning, moving, and disturbing letters I have read was published years ago in a Baptist state paper. A teenager had written to the editor expressing the teen's anger toward the church of which his/her father was pastor. (The letter was not signed.) The writer was bewildered that the church pushed foreign and home missions' offerings but could not see—or did not care—that the pastor was struggling to make ends meet on the salary he received from the church. The breaking point for the teen came after the father had conducted a funeral service in a cold rain and as a result had become ill. He had not been able to afford a topcoat for the winter. The teenager could not understand the reason church members did not see their lack of adequate pay was placing increasing pressure and hardship on the pastor and his family. The teen wrote that because of the father's experience, he/she was finished with Baptist churches.

How many Baptist pastors nervously are staring retirement in the face with the stark realization that they will have a woefully inadequate retirement income and, for some who have lived in church-provided houses, no place to live after retirement? How many pastors have children approaching college age with no way to afford the monumental cost of a college education? Most pastors I have known have not expected to live in luxury, lavishly; they merely have wanted to make a decent living. Churches have the responsibility of providing adequately for their pastors.

6. Churches need to reach and express an understanding that pastors cannot excel in all areas of pastoral leadership. A pastor can be highly skilled in some areas, adequate in others, and weak in still others. When Paul wrote that he was all things to all people (1 Cor. 9:22), he was not pastor of a Southern Baptist church! To be adept in every facet of the pastoral ministry's multiple demands is humanly impossible. I doubt seriously that a pastor exists who excels in preaching, teaching, counseling, administrating, hospital and homebound ministry, staff management, and witnessing. During my long night of crisis, the son of a man to whose family I had ministered extensively and who had turned on me made a statement with which I wholeheartedly agree. The son was a minister of music in a distant Baptist church. In response to his father's complaints against me, the son stated pointedly that pastors have an impossible job. Whether the right word is tolerance, grace, leniency, or understanding, churches must seek to match their ministries with their pastors' strengths. In that way, both can work to bolster the weak areas through skilled laypeople or supportive staffs.

7. Churches can help pastors with their management of time. For conscientious pastors, enough time is not available to get all the work of any one day done. Multiple demands face pastors every day, and one of their tasks is to manage their time for studying; planning; making hospital, nursing-home, homebound, and prospective-member visits; handling emergencies; and counseling.

One way church folk can assist their pastors in the area of time management is to allow them time each day for study, meditation, and prayer. Solid sermon preparation takes many hours a week, 15- to-20 hours per sermon. If the schedules of services call for two sermons on Sunday and at least a devotional or Bible study on Wednesday evenings, unless pastors pull from files of messages they have accumulated they are hard-pressed to meet the weekly demand. In my attempts to study in preparing sermons, I found that a block of hours at the beginning of the work day allowed me to avoid the Late-Saturday-night panic of coming up with sermons for Sunday. Sometimes, Friday afternoon found me finishing up the Sunday evening sermon; but for me, the morning hours were productive, especially when I could begin early.

When pastors indicate their preference of daily blocks of study time, congregations can be made aware of his need so that non-emergency calls, unannounced visits concerning church business matters, and drop-in visits to chat can be made outside the study time. Of course, pastors always will be open to interruptions for emergencies. Yet the congregation's protecting a reasonable block of time for the pastor to prepare for the awesome task of preaching will help him continue to develop in effectiveness. Most Southern Baptist churches demand a great deal in the area of sermon preparation. Three separate preparations a week (during most weeks) calls for a large expenditure of time and energy. Churches' protecting their pastors' time can result in fresh, timely sermons that address the congregations' needs and invite non-Christians to place faith in Christ.

In addition to time for spiritual development and sermon preparation, all pastors need some uninterrupted time each week with their families. One disturbing, growing tragedy is the alarming rate of divorce among pastoral ministers. Numerous elements contribute to the breakup of marriages. To explore these is not within the scope of this book. One factor that contributes to divorce among pastors, however, is their lack of attention to and time with their own families. Many pastors spend countless hours trying to help other couples keep their marriages intact, only to find to their surprise and shock that they have lost their own marriages because they gave too little attention to their wives and children.

Pastors need at least one evening a week they can devote to being with their wives and children. A meal out, a leisurely shopping tour, an out-of-town visit, a family movie—a relaxed evening together at least once a week is vital. Some pastors have set aside Friday evening as being the best and most convenient time to do something special with their families. Churches can render invaluable help in this area by encouraging, even insisting, that their pastors have special times with their families. By doing so, churches will be instrumental in assisting pastors in maintaining healthy relationships at home.

8. Churches can grant and protect vacation time for their pastors each year. Every pastor needs some time away from the multiple pressures of his work, even as other church folk need time away from their normal work routines. Even when pastors take allotted vacation time, they always are subject of being called back for crises that need their attention and ministry. For some, uninterrupted time away is rare and difficult to get. Churches can contribute to their pastors' well-being by providing time away from usual pastoral responsibilities.

Some churches grant study leave for their pastors after the pastors have served for a specified number of years. The length of such study leaves varies, but even a week at a seminary for a continuing theological education conference can renew and refresh pastors. Churches can encourage their pastors to attend, and can provide the means for, such excellent opportunities as personal and professional growth seminars; weeks at conference centers for Bible preaching, pastoral ministry, and Sunday School leadership emphases; and seminary and college extension courses. Any of these offers the possibility of a pastor's increased effectiveness in his work. Exposure to new ideas, helpful books, and fresh approaches to ministry can invigorate pastors and infuse new enthusiasm for their work. As in the case of most other people serious about their jobs or professions, pastors need to "recharge their batteries" periodically. A "sabbatical" or leave is more than a pastoral "perk"; it is an investment in a church's health.

9. Church members consistently can pray for their pastors and let the pastors know they are doing so. Perhaps this and what follows could be placed in the "taken for granted" category, but my guess is that the emphases need to be made periodically in most churches. When they legitimately can do so because of the pastors' ministerial integrity, members of congregations can express their good will toward their pastors as they affirm and encourage them

and join them in the work of ministry that is every Christian's calling.

Pastors and church members have the greatest possible calling, opportunity, and privilege. Under Christ's leading, we can be workers together in the greatest task in the world: being His redemptive body in a world badly in need of redemption. We all are reminded that we are partners; we cannot afford to be adversaries.

Epilogue

In my personal library I have manuals designed to give pastors help in conducting weddings and funerals. One manual includes additional suggestions for baptismal services, Lord's Supper services, parent-child dedication services, and various other dedication and installation services. I have no manual that offers guidance for negotiating the mine-strewn landscape of the pastoral ministry. This little book is not a "how to" manual on pastor/church relations. Neither is it a sure-fire remedy for the deadly epidemic of pastoral terminations now raging. It is designed to draw attention to a needless tragedy being played out almost daily that affects adversely the lives of pastors and churches. Pastoral terminations are not minor events from which pastors and churches move on easily and quickly. Injuries are inflicted that often involve years in recovery, and deaths of ministries frequently occur. Decisions to terminate have serious, lingering, and sometimes fatal consequences.

My chillingly close brush with pastoral termination and my years of reflection on that dark experience in no way qualify me as an expert in pastor-church relations. I have tried to follow my chaplain friend's principle of avoiding giving advice and have been careful to offer suggestions that can be considered and implemented or dismissed. My hope is that these pages have offered some help and encouragement to pastors who courageously struggle on through a long night of pain and wait for the music of renewed, joyful ministry to begin again.